CW00551320

TESTIMONI
PROFIT FIRST for E

"If you want the real nuts and bolts of how to profit from day one in your ecommerce business, you must read this book! So often, as ecommerce entrepreneurs, we have all the drive, product, marketing, and skills needed to make the monster grow, but lack the tools to tame the business and make it serve us and our employees. Cyndi has thoughtfully given us a book that can do just that, and without making our heads swim."

—Jessi Roberts
Owner and brand manager, Cheeky's Brand
Author, *Backroads Boss Lady*

"I have been fortunate to both read Cyndi's book and hear her speak at several ecommerce events. No one is bored when Cyndi starts sharing about accounting and Profit First! What Cyndi teaches is different from what many "guru's" teach about ROI and how to have a successful and profitable ecommerce business. Cyndi knows the ecommerce business better than most CPA's, her advice is solid and if followed can lead to a profitable business. Her experience with using the Profit First system is not just "head knowledge" but something she has used herself and knows from experience that it will work. Both newbies and experienced sellers will have better, stronger and healthier ecommerce businesses if they read and implement the steps outlined in Cyndi's book."

—Carla and Bill Stagg
DS Associates

"*Profit First for Ecommerce Sellers* will literally transform your business overnight by helping you stop guessing about the financial health of your business. This revolutionary approach to managing an online business is the ONLY way to grow a healthy and thriving brand positioned for long-term success in a competitive market. This is a game changer for the ecommerce industry."

—Brandon Andrews
Editor in chief, *The Private Label Insider*
Cofounder, Freedom Shark

"I have talked to a lot of bookkeepers and accountants over the years looking to work with ecommerce sellers. I have found none who have the same level of knowledge and understanding of the challenges of selling online as Cyndi Thomason. The processes she outlines in this book are pure gold and a must-read if you are serious about growing your ecommerce business, especially if you are not analytical by nature."

—Robyn Johnson
CEO, Best From the Nest
Amazon coach and strategic consultant

"*Profit First for Ecommerce Sellers* is a must-read for anyone wanting a profitable ecommerce business from the very start! I've seen this firsthand with members of my E-Commerce Business School community. Cyndi has trained at our events with great success!"

—Ann Sieg
Founder, E-Commerce Business School

"Ecommerce is booming, but ecommerce sellers are struggling. *Profit First for Ecommerce Sellers* will ensure sellers are building their businesses on solid foundations to be profitable in this booming era."

—Skip McGrath
www.SkipMcGrath.com

"Cyndi's knowledge of Profit First and the challenges faced by ecommerce sellers allow her to offer invaluable advice for growing while still putting money in your pocket."

—Andrew Youderian
www.eCommerceFuel.com

"Cyndi Thomason is the rare accountant who looks past the numbers. She'll report accurate and timely financial results to her ecommerce clients. But, more importantly, she'll advise them on how to improve—how to sock money away, reduce stress, and prosper. Smaller ecommerce sellers have to read this book."

—Kerry Murdoch
Publisher, Practical Ecommerce

"*Profit First for Ecommerce Sellers*, in practical terms, explains Cyndi Thomason's proven approach for managing cash flow and profitability. This book is going to help a great many business owners achieve success."

—Paul Grey
Founder of A2X

"Cyndi has fully embraced what it takes to become a true niche accountant in the ecommerce space which enables her to provide ecommerce businesses owners advice at levels above and beyond that of a general practicing accountant/bookkeeper. In this book, Cyndi has successfully taken her ecommerce journey with clients and combined it with the Profit First methodology to create a step by step guide on how to run an ecommerce business that is profitable. Truly proving that #NicheEnablesEverything!"

—David Leary
President, Sombrero Apps Company

The official supplemental Profit First guide for Ecommerce Sellers

PROFIT FIRST

—— *FOR* ——
Ecommerce
Sellers

Transform your ecommerce business from a cash eating monster to a money making machine

CYNDI THOMASON

Introduction by **Mike Michalowicz,** *author of Profit First*

To my daughter, Harris Alaina Thomason:
Your drive to accomplish your goals inspires me daily.

CONTENTS

FOREWORD

by Mike Michalowicz

THE DREAM IS CLEAR: WORK less, make more. The path is just as clear: Sell online.

The biggest entrepreneurial opportunity in the history of mankind is ecommerce. Year after year, more and more people buy online. If ever there was a modern-day gold rush, it is ecommerce. But unlike the gold rush, this one is here to stay. And it is making countless people rich—and, sadly, countless others poor.

That's the strange part. Ecommerce sellers have an opportunity of magnificent proportions, yet so many struggle to create profitable businesses. Maybe that is why you are here now, reading this book. Maybe you too had the dream of growing wealthy from an online business, yet have seen it turn into a cash-sucking, soul-beating nightmare. Or maybe you are doing okay for now, but still falling short of what you have envisioned. If you seek to achieve permanent and predictable ecommerce profitability, you have come to the right place and are about to learn from the right person.

I could never have anticipated the popularity of *Profit First* when I wrote it. Since its publication in 2014, and the subsequent release of the revised and expanded edition in 2016, hundreds of thousands of entrepreneurs have discovered the book. Business owners from every community you could imagine are now using

Profit First in their businesses, from pizza shop owners to pillow manufacturers, from lawyers to doctors, from owners of baseball teams to heads of executive teams, and from leaders in e-health to entrepreneurs in ecommerce.

I wrote *Profit First* to address the needs of all these businesses and more. After the book was published, it quickly became apparent that it was just a foundation for the process of creating profitability. It provided all the core knowledge needed to achieve permanent profitability in business, but it surely didn't address all the nuances of the ecommerce industry. In ecommerce, you must manage special logistics. You must buy inventory. You must deal with the ever-changing fee structure of Amazon, eBay, Etsy, and the other platforms du jour.

Fortunately, you're one of the lucky ones. All the answers you need for your ecommerce business are within these pages. You are about to learn from *the* expert in the industry: Cyndi Thomason. I get a little giddy just saying that. There are many wonderful and highly knowledgeable experts out there, but in my opinion, no one matches the in-depth knowledge, the breadth of experience, and the plain ol' good heart of Cyndi Thomason and her team at bookskeep.

When Cyndi and I sat down to discuss *Profit First* and its impact on ecommerce providers, it was clear: This book is the exact solution you need. In a near-perfectly synchronized outburst, Cyndi and I both exclaimed, "Let's write *Profit First for Ecommerce Sellers*." And so this book was born. Now, with a few adjustments to your approach—complemented by some very specific strategies outlined by Cyndi—you and your fellow ecommerce providers are poised to achieve the business health and wealth you've dreamed about.

This book is a result of over a decade of learning, tweaking, and improving. I conceived *Profit First* in 2008 out of my own desperate need to make my business profitable. It worked. Not just a little bit. It changed my life. Each year that followed, I further simplified the system and introduced it to more and more companies. When I met Cyndi, the entire *Profit First* system had been developed; but I had not specialized it for ecommerce providers. That is what Cyndi has done.

Cyndi has taken *Profit First* and *perfected* it for ecommerce providers. Her leadership in making ecommerce permanently profitable has already benefited thousands through the work of her firm bookskeep, and through her public speaking, her podcasts, and her webinars. She has also personally overseen the rollout of the *Profit First* system for the many ecommerce providers who are fortunate enough to have found a partner in bookskeep. In the process, Cyndi has made *Profit First* her own. She has addressed the unique needs of ecommerce providers, so that you can profitably manage your constantly shifting inventory as well as the constantly shifting requirements of online platforms like Amazon and eBay.

If your sales are increasing while your cash is being depleted, this book will fix that.

If you don't know which of your products make you money and which actually cost you money, this book will answer that.

If you don't pay yourself enough (or anything at all), this book will guide you to finally make the salary you deserve.

Before you dig into *Profit First for Ecommerce Sellers,* I want to share one bit of advice: Take a short break from working in your business and, while you read this, work *on* your business. Beyond just reading this book, do the steps Cyndi has outlined for you.

The only way to experience the results you want is to take decisive action to bring those results about. Cyndi's book is the path to profitability. Let's start walking it now, together.

I wish you much profit, wealth, and happiness in the years ahead.

INTRODUCTION

EVEN IF YOU'VE NEVER SAID it to anyone else, we're going to talk about it. This book is between you and me, and I understand: You don't know if your business is making money or if it ever will make money.

I get it. You're concerned because you never seem to have enough money to pay for the next inventory order. Your friends in Facebook groups and even some coaches advise you to buy more inventory so you'll reach a level that will work. The start-up money is long gone and you're opening more credit card accounts to get the money needed for inventory. You wonder, *Is everyone else doing this? What am I missing? How much longer until we turn the corner?*

This book is about the elephant in the room: Most ecommerce business owners are struggling to make money, and don't have the cash they need to operate.

Mark was mired in this challenge when we first met just before Christmas of 2015. Another year was coming to an end, and he didn't understand his finances. He had no confidence in his data. Mark's business sells products in the fitness category, and he had blindly placed orders for his busy season, Q1. He had tried to get the financial part of his business in order and was disappointed that his fourth bookkeeper was unresponsive. His books were a mess.

This is how I imagine Mark felt then, and how you might sometimes feel, too: You are visiting the grounds of a vast country estate and are in one of those Victorian mazes with the tall hedges. The goal is to find the opening in the hedge so you can get out of maze, where a prize awaits you. It is a race against the clock; you have two minutes, and you're blindfolded. As you scramble through the maze, you bump into the hedges and discover that they have thorns! Will you get out in time, and without being totally bloodied in the process?

Most ecommerce entrepreneurs never imagine they will end up in that maze when they start their journey. Some want to leave the corporate grind; others are simply looking for a change. Many want the flexibility of being able to live anywhere in the world, and to work when they want to work. Some had a need for a product they couldn't find and decided to make their own. Whether you're elbow-deep in managing new product launches or just contemplating dipping a toe into ecommerce to see if it suits you, Amazon's April 2018 shareholder newsletter indicates that you are not alone:

- In 2017, for the first time in Amazon's history, more than half of the units sold on Amazon Marketplace, worldwide, were from third-party sellers.
- In the same year, over 300,000 new US-based small and medium-sized businesses (SMBs) started selling on Amazon.
- Also in 2017, more than 140,000 SMBs saw more than $100,000 in sales on Amazon.
- Amazon sellers come from more than 130 different countries around the world, and from every state in the US.

In *The State of the Amazon Marketplace 2018* report from Feedvisor, we learn that the ranks of the large sellers are growing too: "[T]he number of lucrative, million-dollar sellers has skyrocketed, with Amazon sellers over $1 million gaining 9% of growth versus last year. The number of multimillion-dollar sellers also increased from last year, moving from 1% of sellers in 2017 to 3% in 2018, revealing that these power sellers have established strategies, tactics, and business processes that have allowed them to increase their profits and maintain that growth as they scale and move forward."

So, what's the problem? Why are some ecommerce business owners flourishing, and others frantically wandering around the maze?

The answer is simple: cash flow.

My accounting firm serves ecommerce sellers. Cash flow is always one of the top concerns. It doesn't matter if your business model is private label, wholesale, or retail arbitrage. It doesn't matter if you're running a brand-new start-up with an anticipated yearly revenue of $25,000 or a mature firm with $25 million in yearly revenue. The challenge is the same: make enough money to buy inventory that will generate enough cash to buy more inventory, and hope there's a little left over to pay the owner and make a modest profit.

While the challenge can be easily stated, it's not so easily solved. And what makes matters worse is that—well, I'll admit it—accounting is far from exciting. When faced with learning more about their books and their bottom line, most business owners' eyes glaze over and they tune out. I've been a leader in this business for three years, I genuinely love helping ecommerce entrepreneurs fulfill their dreams, and even I feel like nodding off a few minutes into most accounting trainings and talks.

That changed in October of 2014, when I attended a QuickBooks Connect conference. I sat in a small room at the San

Jose Convention Center, listening to the most boring accounting presentation ever. It was after lunch and, as usual, I was struggling to stay awake. I would drift off and daydream or nod off to sleep, then be brought back to consciousness by a roar of laughter from the conference room next door.

I finally got up the courage to leave my seat and see what was going on in the next room. I caught the last fifteen minutes of Mike Michalowicz's presentation on Profit First. After his talk, he gave out a copy of his newly released book, also called *Profit First*. I didn't hear enough to really want one, but it was free and everyone else in the room was clamoring to get a copy, so I got one too. On the plane ride home, I read the book and was sold on *Profit First*! Understanding Parkinson's law was huge for me. I knew my clients could relate to it; we all use toothpaste. The simplicity of the system, and the fact that it works with our existing behaviors, gave me hope that all my clients could implement it right away.

That conference was a pivotal point for my business. And the subsequent journey for me and the bookskeep team has been amazing. We started with a handful of clients, and today we support nearly one hundred.

As my business grew, I enjoyed helping other entrepreneurs make sense of their companies' finances. But one problem really bothered me. Practically all my clients were struggling with cash flow. I believed there had to be a solution out there, and when I read *Profit First*, I knew I had found that solution. Profit First could help my clients manage their cash flow better. I was determined to figure out how it worked.

To begin, I implemented Profit First in my business. I read the book I was given, and to this day it's filled with the pink sticky notes I used to mark passages I instantly knew I needed to address.

I loved its concepts, and believed that I could make my own little hybrid version work for my business. And I thought that, as an accountant, I could create the accounts within QuickBooks without setting up all the bank accounts.

Within a few weeks, I realized that my approach wasn't working. I was checking the bank balances every morning and not looking at QuickBooks, and as a result my Profit First accounts were invisible and I was back to the same old behaviors. I contacted Ron at Profit First Professionals and decided to get serious. I joined the organization on November 12, 2014. I am one of the first nine people who joined initially and are still active today.

Mike became my business coach when I joined Profit First Professionals. With his guidance, bookskeep narrowed its focus from all small businesses to a specialization in ecommerce. Our first ecommerce client hailed from my home state of Arkansas: Rebecca Wilcox, owner of Rolling T Stores. We began working together in February of 2015. She was my guinea pig, the one who helped me understand the ecommerce business model and how to apply the principles of Profit First. Rebecca had transitioned her business from a rural, brick-and-mortar feed and pet store to an online store offering pet products. She has great private label and bundled wholesale products for dogs. Rebecca and I are both dog lovers, and have shared our love of family, pets, and Rotary exchange programs over the years. Profit First worked for Rebecca. Rebecca is active in many Facebook groups dedicated to ecommerce sellers, and she spread the message about Profit First and how it helped her business.

In a brief time, I picked up several clients in the ecommerce space. I started learning the ropes and discovering some pitfalls. Understanding finance and cash flow is not often part of a small business owner's skillset. As I gained new ecommerce clients,

I realized that few of them were managing their inventory in a sustainable way. Most were so leveraged with debt that they were choking under its weight. I had several clients facing this outcome at the same time. I didn't like taking money from people who were in financial distress. I also didn't like delivering the sad news that their businesses were not profitable, or that their debts were crippling them. I was ready to focus on another industry niche; ecommerce seemed to be nothing but e-promises, empty promises, for my clients. While I wanted to help, I didn't want to be the coroner for the industry, pronouncing business after business dead on arrival.

I began to think that Rebecca was the oddball. Maybe most ecommerce businesses were too highly leveraged. Then I began to work with Mark, who, you might remember, was stuck in the "maze." We worked closely with him to get his financial house in order. Next, we helped him understand the numbers and gain confidence in what they represented. Now he understands his cash flow and can manage it effectively by monitoring his bank account balances. He understands his financial reports and can use them to make informed decisions.

As Mark navigated out of the maze, I went back over our work with Rebecca. What was different with these two clients? Why were they succeeding where so many others were failing? I realized that their success came in part because they avoided the inventory insanity. They had tracked their margins on each and every item. They realized early that it was important to know their numbers so they could make good decisions. Once we sorted out their cash flow issues using Profit First, they had the tools they needed to make their accounting less stressful.

Most ecommerce sellers start out small, the same way I started my business. Is it the same for you? Do you work in a corporate environment or other career but seek flexibility in your time or lifestyle? Do you have small children or aging parents, or want to travel more or feed a neglected entrepreneurial spirit? If so, you are not alone.

The ecommerce industry is one of the greatest opportunities of our time, but it also has a downside. While the barriers to entry are low, the cost to continue to play is buying more inventory. If margins are not consistently above 30 percent, and if inventory spending gets out of hand, the bottom line can go into the red quickly.

The time to start prioritizing profit is now! Don't wait until the hole you've dug is too deep to crawl out. If you make a few simple, strategic moves to ensure profitability starting today, not only will you avoid your company's untimely demise, you will also flourish.

My goal is to give you the path to financial freedom for yourself and your business. It is easier than you think.

In this book, I tell the stories of a mix of entrepreneurs who faced cash flow and other typical ecommerce struggles. Their hard work and attention to process, combined with our Profit First coaching, gave them the skills to successfully navigate perilous ecommerce challenges and emerge with healthy, still-growing businesses.

Mark Brenwall, whom I've already introduced, Carole Rains, and Jeremy Gross are wonderful clients who have graciously agreed to share their stories along with the processes that have led them to positive results. You will learn from their stories that Profit First is not a shazam-and-it's-all-fixed method. It takes dedication and discipline to manage your business so that product launches, inventory reorders, and advertising are in line with your available cash. It requires fortitude to resist the temptation to use debt in ways that will cripple you as you try to repay it and continue to buy inventory. It takes a willingness to stay your course, and resist the appeal of the latest fad coaching program or software subscription, even as others brag about their seven- or nine-digit annual sales. Profit First is not magic. It is a simple, straightforward process that gives you the data you need to manage and grow your business in a sustainable way. And it is oh-so worth it!

Like so many of my clients—and, I suspect, you, too—I founded my business in order to serve the life I was living, and create the life I wanted. I had quit my job to stay home with my daughter as she grew up; I wanted to supplement our income and still have the flexibility to be with her.

You see, whether you're an entrepreneur looking to continue expanding your success by selling products online, or someone entering the world of ecommerce late in life and looking for a new adventure to supplement your income and free up your time to care for loved ones, I understand what motivates you. And I understand that many of you are disillusioned and frustrated. Some of you are even on the verge of financial collapse. I know that's not what you signed up for, and we're going to fix it together.

In this book, I will share the same coaching advice and processes I share with my clients. But beyond my bookskeep clientele, I want all ecommerce sellers to get the finance part of their businesses right. I want you, too, to embrace ecommerce prosperity. So let's get started. It's time to take your Profit First!

Seriously, make the first move and send me an email at Cyndi@ProfitFirstEcom.com. Type "Profit First" in the subject line and tell me what you plan to do with your first profit check!

CHAPTER ONE

The Ecommerce Struggle

IN THIS BOOK, I PROFILE three of my three ecommerce clients, and share stories about how they transformed their businesses into profit-making machines using the Profit First system. While they are very different people, Carole, Mark, and Jeremy have one thing in common: They all love watching Marcus Lemonis in the TV series *The Profit*.

Carole described the show's process to me: "Lemonis always wants to go over the books. He always asks, 'What was your revenue last year? What were your expenses? What's left?' A lot of people are underwater, and it's just amazing to me how many people have virtually no net profit or negative net profit at the end of the year. I can't even imagine that, but it happens all the time, apparently. They just keep putting stuff on credit cards and getting loans."

One aspect of the show that interests Mark is just how appealing ecommerce is when compared to more traditional models. "I watch some of these shows on TV, like *The Profit*, which I love by the way, where they poke around the inside of someone's business. They're running these brick-and-mortar businesses at a 3 percent margin, and I'm just thinking, *This is crazy*. That's the beauty of an online business: the potential to one, have bigger margins, and two, not have the big overhead that you would have with a brick-and-mortar."

Jeremy tunes in to hear the types of questions and concerns Lemonis poses to entrepreneurs. "I immediately think about my own business and how to avoid problems he's talking about, and if I'm doing the right things. Sometimes I find myself thinking similar questions when I walk into a business, such as *How are they making money?* and *Why aren't they doing this easy X Y or Z thing to make this a better customer experience?* And I ask the same 'how are they making money' question *all the time* in the Amazon world when I see sellers dropping prices so low."

Carole, Mark, and Jeremy would do great on *The Profit*. They are using Profit First and their ecommerce businesses are thriving. I wish all my clients had stories with happy endings, but that just isn't the case. As I work with clients, I see many of them struggle as they try to scale their businesses. There are four primary barriers to ecommerce business owners' success:

1. Believing everything will sell during the busy season;
2. Relying on debt to grow a business before a business model is optimized;
3. Lacking basic accounting and financial literacy;
4. And failing to make profitability a focus.

Ecommerce businesses are complex. First, managing inventory is critical, but you can't just look at your shelves and know it's time to reorder. Your inventory could be at any Amazon warehouse, in a prep center, or on a boat from China. Also, there can be huge swings in cash flow depending on the seasonality of your product sales, inventory buildup times, and the need to avoid excessive storage fees. Then there are the unexpected and all-too-frequent occurrences such as inventory lost at the warehouse, account suspensions, or other factors totally outside of your control, all of which require cash to weather. Having firm control of your finances helps you manage and grow your business while enjoying the lifestyle you desire.

In this chapter, I will share more of Carole, Mark, and Jeremy's stories, and take a deeper look at the four main barriers to success.

THE "BUSY" SEASON WON'T PAY OFF YOUR DEBT

MARK, FOUNDER OF eFINITY STUDIOS, has been my client for three years. Like many other ecommerce entrepreneurs, Mark didn't exactly set out with a definite plan in mind. When I asked how he got started, he described his business as "homegrown."

"When I started it in 2014," Mark explained, "I didn't really have any idea about what it was or what it would become. All I knew was, I was hustling to find a way to make steady income. I was pretty successful, consulting for other people and doing some affiliate marketing and things, and I decided to launch one product on Amazon, just to see what that would be like. Four years later, here we are. I still feel like a brand-new beginner at this, although I've had some experience. I've grown a lot."

Mark is a digital nomad. He currently lives in Thailand and travels extensively. Ecommerce affords him this lifestyle, but not everything was optimized when we met. When we first began working together, Mark struggled with his inventory decisions and ran out of stock at crucial times during his busy season. His books were a mess and he had cash flow issues. During his busy season, he had lots of money; then he would run low and rely on his line of credit, or limit his inventory purchases because cash wasn't available.

Many ecommerce sellers are looking for a quick way to make money. They have heard that Amazon businesses can be built and sold in a few years, so they get started, watch their businesses carefully, and make modest profits in their first year. Then, believing more funds can accelerate the process, they begin to rely on credit cards, Amazon loans, or other nonconventional lending to fund inventory purchases.

As sales accelerate, sellers start spending more on operating expenses as they attempt to scale their businesses. The infusion of cash to buy inventory was a temporary bump, and now they must replenish inventory and also pay interest on their debts. This combination of increased operating expenses, accumulating debt, and interest payments can spell serious trouble.

A common belief among my clients is, "Everything will sell during Q4!" Our clients borrow to buy inventory and believe they will pay off their debts with holiday sales. While this can work, I typically see things play out differently. Clients buy late into the season, and their inventory doesn't make it into Amazon warehouses in time to be sold. The items have no appeal in the following months, and are subjected to long-term storage fees as they gather dust. The gross margins were narrow at best, because the clients were not employing sound buying strategies; those narrow margins are then eaten up by fees. A busy season is no guarantee of profitability.

Year two is often a wake-up call. At this point, we dispel the belief that everything will sell at a profit and that borrowing is the way to grow quickly. My clients whose companies are growing profitably tend to grow them using their own cash. Many of them achieved significant growth in two years without relying on debt.

IGNORING FINANCIAL DATA IS A FAST TRACK TO FAILURE

CAROLE RAINS, OWNER OF EMU Joy, was one of our early ecommerce clients. Emu Joy is an all-natural skin and body care business based on the moisturizing and anti-inflammatory properties of emu oil. Emu Joy is sold through its website, on Amazon, and on eBay. Carole's approach to her business is practical, goal-oriented, and definitely seasoned with a little humor.

Carole contacted me after reading *Profit First*, and she was a woman with a plan. She intended to grow Emu Joy and wanted basic bookkeeping services in order to ensure her books were current and clean as a whistle, all with a view to eventually entertaining offers to purchase her company. As we talked, I discovered that Carole also needed a way to easily understand her financial reports and feel confidence in her cash flow decisions.

Our first task was to get her books organized. We started in August, but we updated her books going back to January of that year, which was a big help to Carole. "After a few months with bookskeep, I had a profit and loss statement for the entire year, which was excellent. While having everything in order for taxes is wonderful, I find that the greatest benefit is being able to see my gross margin, my net profit margin, and my whole P&L. Those are the numbers that I look at every month."

Because many of our sellers have come from other careers, they don't understand the need for good financial data or how to interpret financials. And many sellers do not have an accounting system in place, so they often rely on one of the apps that connects with Amazon. I call them "open type" accounting systems. These systems can track some accounting data, but most of them offer no way to reconcile with a statement provided by a financial institution. They can generate a P&L (profit and loss report), but not a balance sheet.

A balance sheet shows the long-term results achieved by the business and gives deeper insight into the company's financial health. Any business that has inventory should be monitoring that inventory on the balance sheet. Inventory is where much of your cash is tied up, and if you don't have a mechanism to understand the value of your inventory, then you won't see the total picture of your business position.

Amazon can take around 30 percent from sales in fees, and far too many sellers don't understand how this impacts their gross margin. Some accountants incorrectly record the deposits as total sales, and this greatly distorts the cost of goods sold and, by extension, gross margin.

In addition, many sellers rely on financial books that are cash-based and report all merchandise purchased as cost of goods sold (COGS). (For a detailed explanation of cash, modified cash, and accrual accounting methods, see our resource page for this book at www.ProfitFirstEcom.com.) This method does not allow you to track the gross margin profitability of sales against the costs of inventory sold on a monthly basis. If sellers are losing money at the gross margin level, they need this information immediately. There are a host of reasons why both reporting and gross margin may be poorly managed, none of which will rescue a company that is bleeding profit. If you are not achieving gross margin profitability, you are not generating enough to fund the Profit First accounts.

Even sellers who can understand a P&L seldom realize the difference between profitability and positive cash flow. There are many accounts that do not show up on the P&L because they are balance sheet accounts. These accounts include inventory, sales tax payable, accounts payable for wholesale or private label orders, and owner/member distributions. The cash required to fund these activities must come from existing bank balances, cash generated from sales, or debt accounts such as loans or credit cards. Since these balance sheet activities do not show up on the P&L, but do affect the amount of cash required to run your business, it is vital to understand the impact they have on your cash position. If you are taking more than the monthly profits from the accounts showing up on the balance sheet, you are living beyond your means for that month.

Accountants can generate a statement of cash flow for you, but Profit First will provide you with an easily understood, real-time system for managing cash so that you won't have to rely on what could be six-week-old data coming from your accountant. Running a profitable ecommerce business absolutely requires you to get a handle on your finances, gross margin, and cash flow.

TO TURN A PROFIT, YOU MUST FOCUS ON PROFIT

I'VE NOTICED THAT MANY ECOMMERCE sellers struggle to maintain focus, an all-too-common problem for entrepreneurs. By nature, entrepreneurs are looking for the next big thing, but starting and growing a business requires a systematic approach with sustained focus on the key drivers of the business. Continuously changing software or training for new approaches takes your attention away from the important revenue-generating aspects of your business.

I can't count the number of ecommerce sellers I've met who've cycled through multiple coaches or mastermind groups, all advising different strategies that are at odds with each other. Many coaches advise that a certain percentage growth or revenue target is a goal. The strategy to get to that goal is based on buying inventory at a certain return on inventory (ROI), and such goals and strategies often suggest plowing all profits back into the business or borrowing money to grow faster. If a potential client is on this path, she is at odds with the basic tenets of Profit First and I have learned that we will not be successful working together. I'm not saying there can't be success in the other approach, just that it is incompatible with Profit First's organic growth pattern, a pattern that has proven to work for my clients.

Mark characterizes himself as a "saver from an early age"; he had the desire to be in better control of his finances, but just didn't have the right tools. To get Mark on the profitability path, we got his books in order, completed a profit assessment, and analyzed his cash flow during a typical month. We set up a checking account for his inventory spending and a savings account for profit in addition to his existing operating expense checking account. As Mark received his payouts from Amazon, he funded his inventory account based on the replenishment costs of the products he just sold. He funded his profit account with 2 percent of his payout. These actions enabled Mark to understand where his cash was going and to set funds aside for the next inventory buy.

By initially putting a small amount in the profit account, he made profit a habit, not an event that occurred at tax time. Once Mark got the hang of the Profit First system, he was off and running.

It's easy to compare your business with other businesses based on what owners report on social media. I've had discovery calls with clients that lead me to expect businesses that are performing well, but when I examine the books, I discover nightmares rather than fairy tales. Entrepreneurs are optimistic by nature, but sometimes their rosy pictures fail to align with current realities.

Profit must be a focus. It must be a habit. I've seen far too many clients struggle and fail in the ecommerce game because they don't focus on what matters most.

PROFIT FIRST SHATTERS BARRIERS TO ECOMMERCE SUCCESS

BEFORE HIS BOOKS WERE IN order, and before he was using Profit First, Mark dealt with daily stresses and frustrations. "I felt like everybody else had it figured out," he explained, "and I was completely lost. I just couldn't find the right person to work as my accounting partner. I found lots of people who told me they could handle my business, but when they got into it, they weren't equipped to help me sort through my challenges and get ready to grow. I had gone through periods of having a very flush bank account, and then all of a sudden, six months later, I was using my line of credit because I hadn't prepared for expenses that were coming up down the road."

Ecommerce businesses need the same basic accounting as traditional retailers. However, the reality of using selling platforms like Amazon, Ebay, and sellers' own websites, coupled with a variety of merchant processors like Paypal and Stripe, is far more complex. When you add in the need to track inventory coming from overseas manufacturers, wholesalers, or clearance outlets, there's enormous opportunity for confusion in the books. You need more than an extra set of eyes to make sure your bank reconciliations come out right, and you can't simply rely on any bookkeeper you find in the phone book. Mark knew he needed more. He wanted to grow eFinity Studios, and he needed an ecommerce specialist who also understood how to prioritize profit.

Much as Mark had, Carole found Profit First to be an enlightening approach to addressing the challenges she faced. She explained how important gross margin is to her, now that she really understands it. "I find that the greatest benefit of having a bookkeeping service is being able to see my gross margin, my net profit margin, and my whole P&L. I look at those numbers every month when I get my report. I think it is extremely important for people to know their percentages. Percentages are more important, really, than knowing what the dollar amount of profit is at the end of the month. It's the percentages that are more telling."

Still others, like Jeremy and Julia Gross, are doing well and simply want to move to the next level. Jeremy and Julia own RubyRoo Baby, an ecommerce business that is focused on Amazon and has a small presence on Shopify, the Walmart marketplace, and a minimal one on eBay. They are in the baby niche, focusing on mostly keepsake items such as baby journals, milestone stickers, and baby shower-related items. Their products are unique because they are inclusive.

"We have Christian, Muslim, Jewish, and Hindu holidays included, and our binding allows you to rip out pages that are not applicable to you," Jeremy explained. "The language we use is inclusive, so it could work for heterosexual couples, homosexual couples, single moms or single dads, or adoptive parents. We put a lot of time into designing for everybody and having it be flexible, kind of like 'choose your own adventure.'"

Jeremy had their financial books in order and was successfully managing inventory, but he wanted to make the transition from part-time Amazon seller with a full-time day job to working in his business full-time with no other income source. Jeremy's challenge was to find a way to generate enough income from RubyRoo that he could enjoy spending more time with his wife and young children. We worked together and used Profit First to set up an owner pay account that, after about six months, allowed him to make that jump to full-time ecommerce seller and more present family man. He has particularly appreciated this flexibility in the past few months as extended family across the country have had health issues.

Carole, Mark, and Jeremy figured it out, and so can you. You are not alone. And no matter the choices you made in the past, or the challenges you are facing now, you can do this. I know it's possible, because I've helped people dig themselves out of holes so deep they couldn't see the light. You may think your challenges are insurmountable, but I promise you, they are not. I'm going to say this one more time, because I don't just believe in the Profit First system, I believe in you. Yes, you can do this. Let's get started.

———

NOW IT'S YOUR TURN. ARE you ready to take the steps necessary to be permanently profitable? Get started today! Download our Quick Start Guide at www.ProfitFirstEcom.com.

CHAPTER TWO

Profit First, Engineered for Ecommerce

In the previous chapter, we talked about the four common barriers to success commonly faced by ecommerce sellers. The Profit First system is your solution for all four! Based on our clients' experience, my team and I set out to customize Profit First for our clients and ultimately the ecommerce industry. We set up the system specifically for you.

The principles of Profit First stay untouched. It is a sturdy and powerful approach to growing your business. The foundation and methods are recapped in this book in an abbreviated form so that you have everything in one spot. See the gray boxes throughout. And, if you want to dig deeper into the core system, I encourage you to read the bible itself: *Profit First: Transform your Business from a Cash-Eating Monster to a Money-Making Machine*. Or snag the audiobook if you'd rather listen and hear Mike's legendary energy around the concept, as well as some additional stories not found in the book.

The Profit First solution doesn't attempt to change who you are or how you behave. That is impossible. The solution sets up a system that channels your existing behavior toward the outcome that serves you.

OVERVIEW OF THE PROFIT FIRST SYSTEM

THE FOUR CORE PRINCIPLES
OF PROFIT FIRST

Let's take a moment to talk dietary science. No groans, please. This stuff is fascinating.

In 2012, a report by Koert Van Ittersum and Brian Wansink in the *Journal of Consumer Research* concluded that the average plate size in America had grown 23 percent between the years 1900 and 2012, from 9.6 inches to 11.8 inches. Running the math, the article explains that should this increase in plate size encourage an individual to consume just fifty more calories per day, that person would put on an extra five pounds of weight each year. Year after year, that adds up to a very chunky monkey.

But using smaller plates is just one factor. A Twinkie on a small plate is still a Twinkie. There is more to a healthy diet, and it is based on four core principles of weight loss and nutrition.

1. **Use Small Plates**—Using smaller plates starts a chain reaction. When you use a small plate, you get smaller portions, which means you take in fewer calories. When you take in fewer calories than you normally would, you start to lose weight.
2. **Serve Sequentially**—If you eat the vegetables, rich in nutrients and vitamins, first, they will start satisfying your hunger. When you move on to the

next course—your mac and cheese or mashed potatoes (they don't count as veggies!)—you will automatically eat less. By changing the sequence of your meals by eating your vegetables first, you automatically bring a nutritional balance to your diet.

3. **Remove Temptation**—Remove any temptation from where you eat. People are driven by convenience. If you're anything like me, when there's a bag of Doritos sitting in the kitchen, it calls out to you constantly—even when you aren't hungry. If you don't have any junk food in the house, you're probably not going to run out to the store to get it. (That would mean putting on pants.) You're going to eat the healthy food you stocked instead.

4. **Enforce a Rhythm**—If you wait until you are hungry to eat, it is already too late and you will binge. Then you are likely to eat too much and stuff yourself. You go from starving to stuffed, and back to starving again. These peaks and valleys in your hunger results in way too much calorie consumption. Instead, eat regularly (many researchers suggest five small meals a day) so that you never get hungry. Without the peaks and valleys, you will actually eat fewer calories.

Though they don't realize it, the folks in the diet industry know quite a lot about growing a healthy business. Here's how you apply the four principles:

1. **Use Small Plates**—When money comes into your main INCOME account, it simply acts as a serving

tray for the other accounts. You then periodically disperse all the money from the INCOME account into different accounts in predetermined percentages. Each of these accounts has a different objective: one is for profit, one for owner compensation, another for taxes, and another for operating expenses. Collectively, these are the five foundational accounts (Income, Profit, Owner's Comp, Tax, and Operating Expenses), and where you should get started, but advanced users will use additional accounts.

2. **Serve Sequentially**—Always, *always* allocate money based upon the percentages to the accounts first. Never, ever, ever pay bills first. The money moves from the INCOME account to your PROFIT account, OWNER'S COMP, TAX, and OPEX (OPERATING EXPENSES). Then you pay bills only with what is available in the OPEX account. No exceptions. And if there isn't enough money left for expenses? This does *not* mean you need to pull from the other accounts. What it *does* mean is that your business is telling you that you can't afford those expenses and need to get rid of them. Eliminating unnecessary expenses will bring more health to your business than you can ever imagine.

3. **Remove Temptation**—Move your PROFIT account and other "tempting" accounts out of arm's reach. Make it really hard and painful to get to that money, thereby removing the temptation to "borrow" (i.e., steal) from yourself. Use an accountability mechanism to prevent access, except for the right reason.

4. Enforce a Rhythm—Do your allocations and payables twice a month (specifically, on the tenth and twenty-fifth). Don't pay only when there is money piled up in the account. Get into a rhythm of allocating your income, and paying bills twice a month so that you can see how cash accumulates and where the money really goes. This is controlled recurring and frequent cash flow management, not by-the-seat-of-your-pants cash management.

To put the Profit First principles into practice, you open multiple bank accounts for specific purposes. Below is a recap from the book detailing the five foundational accounts. The accounts are included here for reference, but we have created a modified structure for our ecommerce clients. Chapter Four gives you all the details about the accounts that work best for ecommerce businesses.

THE FIVE FOUNDATIONAL ACCOUNTS

What you are about to do is the foundation of Profit First. This is the structure your profits will be built on. All the muscle in the world is useless if it isn't connected to a strong skeletal structure. These accounts are the bones. Here are the five checking accounts you need to set up:

1. INCOME
2. PROFIT

3. OWNER'S COMPENSATION
4. TAX
5. OPEX

Make sure you set these up as checking accounts. The flexibility offered by checking accounts far outweighs any minuscule interest you get by using savings accounts. Call your bank and set up the foundational five accounts. Most banks allow you to assign a nickname to the account that is displayed online and on statements in addition to the account number. Just as Mom labeled her envelopes, name your accounts according to their purpose.

You can use your existing primary bank account as one of the five accounts. Rename it your OPEX (a popular abbreviation for Operating Expenses) account because you are likely paying all your bills from that account. Going forward, we are just going to move deposits to your INCOME account. That should be a no-brainer for check deposits; simply put them into a new account. For other types of deposits, such as credit card or ACH payments, you'll have to update your bank information wherever necessary. The process will take about half an hour—if you have a lot of automated payments, maybe an hour. Make the effort and get this done.

The Profit First framework works for all businesses. But it is just that: a framework. Our firm has taken this foundation and built a structure specifically for ecommerce sellers. With these few additional techniques, you will position your business for permanent profitability. I'll go into greater detail in subsequent chapters, but briefly, ecommerce sellers should make the following changes:

1. Don't set up a separate income account if 80 percent or more of your revenue is from Amazon or some other marketplace and you receive your payouts biweekly. Basically, Amazon is functioning as your income account by holding your money for two weeks. In this case, your Amazon deposit can go directly into your operating expense account and you can transfer the funds from that account.

2. Open a separate checking account for inventory. Profit First works with real revenue, which, as Mike describes it, is the funds available after you have paid for your materials and subcontractors. In an ecommerce business, this is your inventory and inventory-related items such as your prep or fulfillment center. If you are in retail arbitrage, it would also include your shoppers. Before you jump into your Profit First accounts and start allocating your real revenue, you must ensure that you have good control of your inventory cash flow, which means separating it into an account that we can monitor closely.

3. Make adjustments for seasonality. Most of our clients have seasonal fluctuations in their sales. Typically, sellers see a big bump in sales during Q4, though sellers in the fitness and diet niche peak in Q1, while golf and gardening products peak in Q2. Implementing Profit First in a seasonal business has some unique challenges. We must factor in the seasonal sales cycle as we develop our Profit First strategy. Chapter Six will explain how seasonality can work for you to improve your profitability.

PROFIT ASSESSMENT: HOW HEALTHY IS YOUR BUSINESS?

Now that you have a basic understanding of the Profit First system, let's examine your business through the lens of Profit First. Looking at your business compared with benchmark numbers from healthy businesses can cause you to take off the rose-colored glasses and get real... or not. Believe it or not, I've had many clients look at the numbers, say, "Yeah, this doesn't surprise me" and continue down the same path. Most of the time I hear from them later, when they don't have many options because of their debt. It takes real courage to look at the numbers, face the facts, and get busy making your business better.

I'm betting you have the courage and the desire to tackle your cash-eating monster. You may not have numbers for all of the categories such as profit, owner pay, or taxes, but don't worry— that's why we're doing this exercise. I'm going to show you how to complete your profit assessment. If you're concerned about completing this step, stop now and watch the video tutorial I have prepared for you. You will find it on our resources page at www.ProfitFirstEcom.com. Once you are ready to dive in, gather these items from your financial records*:

1. Balance sheets from the last month of prior year-end and the most recent prior month-end. Print this out by year so you see a column for the prior year and a column for year-to-date in the current year. Export this information into an Excel spreadsheet if you can. Start with the current year-to-date account balances and subtract the prior year's account balances. The resulting difference will be used in our assessment.

2. Profit and loss, year-to-date through prior month-end.

*Note: I am assuming a calendar year end and cash books, or modified cash where inventory purchases hit the balance sheet and entries are made to the P&L for COGS. If your fiscal year-end date is different, you need to adjust the dates so you can compare the prior year-end numbers with the last completed month of the current year. Be sure the time period you choose for the P&L and the balance sheet is the same. For illustration purposes, I'm going to examine records from January—June, 2018. This will require us to pull a P&L for the period January—June 2018 and a balance sheet from December 31, 2017 to June 30, 2018 with columns for each year (2017 and 2018). See the example below.

This is the profit assessment form you will be completing:

	ACTUAL	PP%	PF$	THE BLEED	THE FIX
Top Line Revenue					
Inventory					
Real Revenue		100%			
Profit					
Owner's Pay					
Tax					
Operating Expenses					

Below is a description for each box to help you derive each number you will need as you complete the chart. I have also prepared an example of a completed chart and example work papers. You can find them after the descriptions for each box. If the thought of this task has your heart racing and your palms sweating, take a few minutes now to check out my video tutorial at www.ProfitFirstEcom.com.

Top Line Revenue: This is the total revenue from your P&L.

Inventory: From your balance sheet worksheet, the difference number for your inventory account between December and June. That number will be added to your COGS number on your P&L.

Real Revenue: This is top line revenue less inventory.

Profit: Look at your balance sheet and take the difference number you calculated for your cash bank accounts. If you have more money in your bank now than you had at the end of the year, this will be a positive number; if you have less, this will be a negative number. Then look at your liabilities. What you owe on credit cards, lines of credit, and Amazon or Kabbage loans must be considered. Take the difference number you calculated and subtract that from the number you calculated for your bank accounts. This is where it gets hard, because if you pay off your credit cards each month, you may still have a negative profit account number. I often see people that expect future sales to pay their credit cards. This means they have negative real profit, even though they pay off their credit cards each month and the bottom line on their P&L is positive.

Owner's Pay: You may find this in the salary number on your P&L, or you may find it as an owner distribution on the balance sheet, or both. If you are taking both, add the difference number you calculated for the balance sheet to the salary number from the P&L.

Tax: This is only for state and federal income taxes—not sales tax or franchise taxes, which stay in operating expenses. If you are paying estimated taxes, you should find this on your balance sheet. If you are recording estimated taxes on the P&L, use that number.

Operating Expenses: Start with the expense total from your P&L. Reduce the total by any owner's pay or taxes that are included in that number.

After you have added all this information into the form, take the top line revenue and subtract inventory, profit, owner's pay, tax, and operating expenses from that number. It should equal zero or be close. If it doesn't, then go back and double-check your numbers. Look specifically at the balance sheet. You want to be sure you used the difference calculation for all numbers pulled from the balance sheet. If you used your June year-end number, it will not give you a proper result. Sometimes, too, there can be an error in the signs when you make your calculations. Also, be sure that every asset, liability, and owner distribution/contribution account that has changed on the balance sheet is represented in your calculations.

The last step is to translate your profit, owner's pay, tax, and operating expenses as percentages of real revenue. Take each number, i.e. profit, divide it by the real revenue number, and then multiply by 100 to get a percentage: Profit / real revenue x 100 = Profit First percentage. Add this to your table.

Once you have completed your table, you may have some rows left blank. You may not be paying yourself or paying estimated taxes. Compare your chart with the percentages from a healthy business. Below is the chart that Mike Michalowicz presents in *Profit First*. This chart was developed based on Mike's research of thousands of healthy businesses.

	A	B	C	D	E	F
Real Revenue Range	$0 - $250k	$250k - $500k	$500k - $1m	$1m - $5m	$5m - $10m	$10m - $50m
Real Revenue	100%	100%	100%	100%	100%	100%
Profit	5%	10%	15%	10%	15%	20%
Owner's Pay	50%	35%	20%	10%	5%	0%
Tax	15%	15%	15%	15%	15%	15%
Operating Expenses	30%	40%	50%	65%	65%	65%

EXAMPLES OF COMPLETED PROFIT ASSESSMENT AND WORK PAPERS

IN THE PROFIT ASSESSMENT, NOTE that the top line revenue for this business falls within Column B on the chart above. That is where the PF%s come from in the chart. The PF$ is the amount for each category and is calculated based on the PF% multiplied by actual real revenue. The rest of the numbers are taken from the P&L and balance sheet examples that follow. The bleed is the difference based on the actual column compared to the PF$ and represents the opportunity for this business to improve.

	Actual	Actual %	PF %	PF$	The Bleed	The Fix
Top Line Revenue	611,428					
Inventory	138,125					
Real Revenue	473,303	100%	100%	473,303		
Profit	19,095	4.03%	10.00%	47,330	28,235	increase
Owner's Pay	74,810	15.81%	35.00%	165,656	90,846	increase
Tax	-	0.00%	15.00%	70,995	70,995	increase
Operating Expense	379,268	80.13%	40.00%	189,321	(189,947)	decrease

Verification   129   Real Revenue less Profit less Owner's Pay less Tax less OpEx
% off   0.02% Verification # divided by Top Line Revenue
                          Don't worry about if less than 5%

Balance Sheet
As of June 30, 2018

	Dec 31, 2017	Jan - Jun, 2018	Difference	
ASSETS				
Current Assets				
Total Bank Accounts	5,127	37,072		
Other Current Assets				
Amazon Carried Balances	483	613		
Inventory	100,524	95,524		
Total Other Current Assets	101,007	96,137	(4,871)	
Total Current Assets	106,135	133,209		
TOTAL ASSETS	106,135	133,209	27,074	Change in Assets less change in Inventory - Change in Liabilities
LIABILITIES AND EQUITY				
Liabilities				
Current Liabilities				
Total Credit Cards	24,999	41,454		
Other Current Liabilities				
Total Loans Payable	115,284	116,503		
Sales Tax Payable	4	50		
Total Other Current Liabilities	115,288	116,553		
Total Current Liabilities	140,287	158,007		
Total Liabilities	140,287	158,007	17,720	14,225 Profit
Equity				
Owner's Contribution		27,836	27,836	(32,250) Owner Pay = Owner Contribution less Owner Draw plus salary on P&L; final number on P&L
Owner's Draw	(135,244)	(134,676)	(60,086)	
Retained Earnings	568	568	568	
Net Income	568	46,604	46,036	
Total Equity	(134,676)	(120,322)	14,354	
TOTAL LIABILITIES AND EQUITY	5,611	37,685	32,074	

Profit and Loss
January - June, 2018

	Total	
Income		
Total **AMZ** Product Charges	78,695	
EDI Pymnts	4,091	
Total **PayPal Sales**	107,685	
Sales of Product Income (non-eCom)	4,329	
Total **Stripe Sales**	416,628	
Total Income	**611,428**	Top Line Revenue
Cost of Goods Sold	39,234	
Total Cost of Sales	103,761	
Total Cost of Goods Sold	**142,995**	138,125 Total COGS plus change in Inventory from Balance Sheet
Gross Profit	**468,432**	
Expenses		
Total **Advertising/Promotion**	99,328	
Total **Bank Charges/Fees**	(978)	
Charitable Contributions	25	
Commissions	60,627	
Computer/Internet	4,044	

Contract Labor	2,257	
Dues/Subscriptions	26,033	
Gifts/Donations	454	
Insurance	(22)	
Total Interest Paid	13,827	
Legal/Professional Fees	26,277	
Meals/Entertainment	4,333	
Office Expenses	2,428	
Total Payroll Expenses	106,984	42,560 Owner Pay in Payroll; from payroll register information
Postage	24	32,250 Net of Owner Contribution and Owner Draw On Bal Sheet
Product/Market Development	169	74,810 Owner Pay
Rent	23,695	
Telephone Expenses	1,989	
Training/Education	8,298	
Travel	14,503	
Utilities	1,602	
Total Expenses	**395,898**	
Net Operating Income	**72,535**	
Total Other Income	0	
Total Other Expenses	25,931	
Net Other Income	**(25,931)**	
Net Income	**46,604**	

How do you compare? Don't be discouraged if your numbers are low or nonexistent for profit, owner's pay or taxes. Hang in there! The first step in changing your company's financial future is doing the initial assessment. Once you know your numbers, I'll show you how you can create a course of action.

If your business is more complicated, and you're having trouble making sense of the numbers and plugging in the right figures, don't worry. I have a tutorial for just this scenario on my website: www.ProfitFirstEcom.com. *Profit First* is also a great resource that gives you much more detail, and if you're still stuck, just reach out to my team at cyndi@ProfitFirstEcom.com and we'll be happy to help you figure it out.

A profit assessment is a great tool to get the 50,000-foot view of your business. It gives you a sense of the general topography of your business and allows you to benchmark against other businesses of a comparable size. Most of our ecommerce clients, however, have big seasonal fluctuations in their businesses. Many are looking to capitalize on the Christmas season and Q4 is huge for them. Others in the fitness industry benefit from New Year's resolutions, and Q1 is their peak season. Those selling outdoor products like golf clubs and garden supplies make their largest sales in Q2. When you complete your profit assessment, you are typically reviewing your business financials for a full year. The fact that 75 percent of your sales occur in a specific quarter skews the results of the assessment. As a result, the allocation percentages suggested in the assessment using sales that include the biggest sales quarter will cause your percentages to be high, and you may not be able to sustain these percentages if you are starting Profit First during your slow season.

To ensure that we start with sustainable target allocation percentages, we need to understand cash flow during a typical month. How much do you need to set aside to replenish your inventory? How will setting those funds aside impact your operating expenses? Many ecommerce sellers fund their daily operations with cash from sales. They do not set funds aside to replenish inventory and, as a result, must rely on credit cards, Amazon loans, or factoring-type capital. It is a very expensive and becomes a cycle, one that can be nearly impossible to escape.

MONTHLY CASH FLOW SPREADSHEET

To perform a cash flow analysis, we developed a monthly cash flow spreadsheet to capture the cash transactions and model the target allocation percentages required to meet the cash requirements for inventory, owner's pay, taxes, and operating expenses. This monthly cash flow spreadsheet examines one month of cash transactions during a typical sales month, not during your high season. We create a baseline of operations for your business from there.

Because your Amazon payouts are net of fees, we use the net payout amount, not the actual product sales, for this cash flow analysis. This is different from our approach to bookkeeping or accounting. To understand your profitability and trends in the business from an accounting perspective, we want to ensure that all the activity that occurs at Amazon is recorded on your books. From a cash flow perspective, we are concerned with the net amount that is deposited in the bank account and available for allocation to our Profit First accounts. This makes administering the system easier for you.

It is important to note that, once the monthly cash flow spreadsheet is complete and the target allocation percentages are determined, these percentages will not match the percentages on the profit assessment. The profit assessment calculates percentages based on real revenue. In this type of analysis, the Amazon fees would be deducted from the top line revenue along with the inventory expenses. We're using a hybrid approach to facilitate biweekly processing of your Amazon deposit. We're going to take the Amazon payout (net of fees) as our real revenue and calculate the target allocation percentages for inventory, profit, owner's pay, taxes, and operating expenses. See the example below.

Step 1: Download your bank transactions.

To complete this process, you will use the transactions from all of your bank and credit card accounts. Within your accounting system, it is easy to download these transactions into a spreadsheet. We will show you how to do that in a video tutorial that you can access at the end of this chapter.

Step 2: Complete box 1 for income.

Simply cut and paste the deposits into box 1 in either of the two columns depending on the date. You will note that this spreadsheet mirrors the dates Mike recommends in Profit First, the 26th and 10th and 11th and 25th (more on that in Chapter Six). You will have an Amazon payout during each of these periods. Do not use a month that has three payouts.

Step 3: Complete boxes 2 and 3 with your expenses.

Look at your expenses and add each to box 2 or 3 based on the date of the expense and the proper column within box 2 or 3 based on the type of expense. The spreadsheet has columns for operating expenses, inventory, owner pay, and taxes in order to calculate the actual amount you are paying into these Profit First buckets.

Step 4: Perform a what-if analysis.

Once you have added all your expenses, go back to box 1 where your revenue is recorded. Add and adjust your percentages to ensure that the income can be spread to cover all actual expenses calculated from boxes 2 and 3. When you adjust the percentages, the spreadsheet will calculate the dollar amount allocated based on your income multiplied by the percentage. Compare that to the actual expense totals recorded from boxes 2 and 3. Adjust the percentage up or down until you get close to the actual amount. If your income is less than your total expenses, you need to determine why. Did you buy a lot of inventory that will provide you with stock for many months? If so, divide that actual inventory amount by the number of months it will cover. If you are overspending on operating expenses, then you will see the impact of those purchases on the level of your income. It's time to get serious about reducing expenses.

Monthly Cash Flow for _____ **Client Name**

Input	Calculate

1. Income and Allocations

Regular Income		Income for Period			
		26 - 10	11 - 25	Total	Actual
				$	
				$	
				$	
				$	
Total Income	$	$	$	$	
Quarterly Target Allocation %					
	Inventory	$	$	$	$
	Profit	$	$	$	$
	Taxes	$	$	$	$
	Owner Pay	$	$	$	$
	Operating Expense	$	$	$	$
	(Should equal 100%)	$	$	$	$
Drip Income					
Months	Amount				

Instructions:

Make a copy of the Master Template and insert it immediately to the left of the Master Template tab. Change that tab name and make the header setup entries.

Box 1) Add your Quarterly Target Allocation Percentages. Add the income you receive based on the dates - either 26-10 or 11-25. Input total amount of special "Drip Income" in Drip Income Amount cell. Designate number of months over which to apply the income in the Drip Income Periods cell.

Box 2 and 3) Add the typical monthly expenses depending on the date you will pay it.

As you adjust your income, Target Allocations and expenses, your remaining balance will be displayed in Box 4 so you can begin to understand the variables at play and adjust expense payments to ensure you maintain a positive cash flow. Make notes for your records then copy the Worksheet over for the following month.

4. Month-end Remaining Balance Total	$0.00

2. Expense Tracking Period (26-10)

Operating Expense Allocation	$
Other Income	
Insert above this row	
Income (26-10)	$

Operating Expense Allocation	$
Other Income	
Insert above this row	
Income (26-10)	$

Day	Vendor Payment	Amount	Inventory	Owner Pay	Taxes	Operating Expenses
Total Expenses (26-EOM)	$	$	$	$	$	
Remaining Balance (26-EOM)		$0.00				

Day	Vendor Payment	Amount	Inventory	Owner Pay	Taxes	Operating Expenses
Total Expenses (11 - 25)	$	$	$	$	$	
Remaining Balance (11 - 25)		$0.00				

Day	Vendor Payment	Amount	Inventory	Owner Pay	Taxes	Operating Expenses
Total Expenses (1 - 10)	$	$	$	$	$	
Remaining Balance (26-EOM)		$0.00				

Notes:

QUICK START

SOMETIMES THE BEST WAY TO start is just to start! If you own a new business, you have no history to work with and will not know your percentages. Even if you've been in business for a few years, you may not have good financial data. Or you may not like working with numbers and feel overwhelmed at the prospect of completing the assessments. Don't wait if you're new, and don't let analysis paralysis put you off. Jump in and begin by adding a checking account for inventory and a savings account for profit. Just having these two accounts in addition to your operating expense account will start you on the right path.

Take a look at Chapter Four for how to move money into your inventory account. It's a simple process that will give you great insight into your business. Then move 1 percent of your payout each month into your profit account. Each quarter, try to reduce operating expenses 1 percent and move that savings into your profit account. With these simple steps, you will build a profitable business.

TAKE ACTION

ROLL UP YOUR SLEEVES AND let's dig in! The profit assessment tutorial and the monthly cash flow spreadsheet and tutorial are available for you to download at www.ProfitFirstEcom.com

CHAPTER THREE

Stop the Inventory Insanity

SOME ECOMMERCE SELLERS ENTER THE business believing that inventory is straightforward and easy to understand. It ain't that simple, and many sellers go belly-up because they never get a handle on how to manage inventory in a profitable way. An easy way to begin to better understand your inventory is to use a separate bank account for all your inventory-related purchases. Simply separating out your inventory funds is an important step toward being able to replenish inventory without borrowing money and without using money designated for other purposes. This strategy relies on Parkinson's Law, which is the basis of the "small plates" principle.

PARKINSON'S LAW

In 1955, a modern philosopher named C. Northcote Parkinson came up with the counterintuitive Parkinson's Law: that the demand for something expands to match its supply. In economics, this is called induced demand—it's why expanding roads to reduce traffic congestion never works in the long term because more drivers always show up in their cars to fill those extra lanes.

Similarly, if your client gives you a week to turn around a project, you'd likely take the whole week—but if she gives you just a day, you'll make it happen in a day. You see, the more we have of something, the more of it we consume. This is true for anything: food, time, even toothpaste.

Isn't it funny how much we change based upon what is available? Here is what's fascinating: Parkinson's Law triggers two behaviors when supply is scant. When you have less, you do two things. The first is obvious: you become frugal. When there is less toothpaste in the tube, you use less to brush your teeth. That is the obvious part. But something else, far more impactful happens: you become extremely innovative and find all sorts of ways to extract that last drop of toothpaste from the tube.

If there is one thing that will forever change your relationship with money, it is the understanding of Parkinson's Law. You need to intentionally make less toothpaste (money) available to brush your teeth (to operate your business). When there is less, you will automatically run your business more frugally (that's good) and you will run your business far more innovatively (that's great!).

Carole, an early adopter of Profit First, agreed right away with the need for a separate account for inventory. She explained, "We decided to add an additional account just for inventory. Initially there was only a single account for expenses, which is how Mike has it set up in the basic Profit First methodology.

For me, it felt like inventory was too big a number to just lump in with all the other expenses. It helps especially when you've got seasonal products. You build the balance up so that there's plenty of money to buy inventory when you need to ramp up for the season.

"The other thing I really like about having inventory and operating expenses separate is that it keeps me from spending willy-nilly on all kinds of potential marketing opportunities. There's tons and tons of ways I could spend money on advertising and promotions."

Carole found right away that having that separate account kept her focused when it came to spending. The inventory account is sacred, because without inventory, there's nothing to sell!

Inventory in general is challenging for clients. Mark described his biggest issue as an Amazon seller: "The number one issue I've faced since I've started has been inventory management. Surprisingly, learning how to find a product, get it made in China, do the quality control, get things shipped to America, or whatever country I'm selling in at the time… that stuff has been pretty easy overall.

"Certainly, there are little issues here and there, but the big nuts to crack for me have always been how to order enough or not order too much and how to predict how much money I'm going to need to fill the warehouse. Those are the things I still struggle with. Planning for Christmas—how soon do I need to start increasing my orders? How much do I have to order? How are my sales going to be? These are things that you only get after years of data. Now I feel like I probably have enough data to make smarter decisions. But still, it's sort of a struggle."

Mark points out a hidden benefit of Profit First, one that's particularly useful for ecommerce sellers. He notes that it's data—good, reliable, long-term data—that empowers us to make better business decisions. With its small plates approach, Profit First makes slicing and dicing that data simpler.

Much is outside our control when it comes to inventory, so it's smart to focus on what we can control. In this chapter, we're going to concentrate first on the cash flow aspects of inventory management. If you're starting out with a new business, you have the perfect opportunity to start out right. Presumably, you have some initial capital that you used to fund your initial inventory buy. With the first payout, you should set aside funds to replenish your inventory. The amount you set aside will be based on the total cost of the products you just sold. If you need help determining the cost of your products, we have a spreadsheet template that you can download to ensure that you consider all costs. You can find it at www.ProfitFirstEcom.com. Most of our clients are using either a spreadsheet or a software as a service (SaaS) inventory solution such as Inventory Lab, Teikametrics, Skubana, or Seller Cloud, to name several.

When you receive a payout from Amazon, you will calculate the inventory cost of the items sold during the payout period, and you will move these dollars into your inventory bank account. You repeat this process with every Amazon payout. After two or three months, you can set a target allocation percentage using the monthly cash flow spreadsheet. For the first few months, do the actual calculation to get a feel for your numbers.

ROI, GROSS MARGIN, AND ECONOMICS OF ONE UNIT

EXPERIENCED SELLERS KNOW INVENTORY IS complex. How do you know which products to sell? What will it cost you to acquire the products? How much inventory do you start with? How should you price your products, and where do you get the capital to fund those inventory buys? Unlike a traditional retailer, you often won't see the products you are selling. All the tactile data points are missing if you're using a wholesale or private label business model. Fortunately, Amazon and most other ecommerce business platforms provide lots of data to help you. But what data should you pay attention to? A cottage industry has cropped up for Amazon coaches who can help you navigate the maze of managing inventory.

Robyn Johnson, CEO of Best from the Nest, is a Profit First Professional Amazon coach. She and I collaborate frequently, and her contributions are priceless. Her advice is, "When sourcing, look for products that have an ROI of at least 40 percent and slowly raise that to 50-70 percent as you get more skilled. This means you will spend more time sourcing than some of your counterparts that are looking for lower returns on inventory (ROIs). Watch your gross margins to ensure that your repricing software and other costs of sales have not eroded your profit margin. Also consider the economics of one unit to ensure that each product is contributing to cover your operating costs."

Robyn covers a lot in her typically insightful, rapid-fire fashion, so let's break it down and make sure we glean every bit of wisdom. First let's examine ROI. Amazon sourcing apps look at an item and make comparisons between it and other products currently being sold on Amazon. You enter your cost to purchase the product and it will calculate the estimated Amazon fees and suggest a selling price based on the current selling price of the same product. Based on the typical sales price, cost of the product, and fees, the app can give you an estimated profit on that product. This is your ROI. To calculate ROI manually, you take the profit of the product and divide it by cost of the product, then multiply this by one hundred to get a percentage.

(Product's Profit/Cost of Product) x 100 = ROI%

This calculation is net of Amazon fees. When you make this calculation at the time you are considering purchasing the unit to sell, you need to be realistic in estimating your selling price.

Evaluate your ROI in several different scenarios:

1. At the product level;
2. At the portfolio level, encompassing all products;
3. At the product level for the products that make up the top 10 percent of revenue; and
4. At the product level for the products that make up the bottom 10 percent of revenue.

Understanding ROI for your entire portfolio is important if you are trying to gauge which products will bring you a return great enough to help fund your operating expenses. It is too easy to get excited about a single product that shows 80 percent ROI and believe it will carry through and boost the overall portfolio. Below is an example of a client's ROI for the products that make up the top 10 percent of revenue. This client told me his buying strategy was an ROI of 80 percent, and was concerned that the gross margin on his books was much lower, at 20 percent. When I examined the ROI data, it was clear that he was using the ROI of a few products that achieved 80 percent ROI to paint the entire portfolio that had only a 33 percent ROI in total. This was much closer to the gross margin.

ROI Profit / Direct Cost

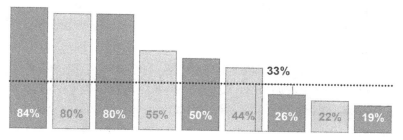

While this example is for one client, it is a common concern we hear when we clean up books for clients. They have an expectation regarding the ROI number, and when we present the books, the gross margin number is usually significantly lower. There are many reasons for this gap. The first is illustrated by the client example above. This client used a few good ROI products and painted the entire portfolio with this broad brush. Secondly, the inventory system used to track ROI may not include all the costs if they are manually calculated and loaded in the system.

Most inventory systems rely on direct data input, which means data are not tied back to source documents. This leaves room for calculation and transcription errors. It is easy to forget the cost of shipping or packaging, for example. Accounting system transactions are traced back and reconciled with outside statements provided by your financial institution, and this reconciliation step ensures they are accurate.

Finally, ROI calculations are typically made at the time of purchase, and repricing the product over the time it is sold will give you a different actual ROI. If you are using ROI to make major purchasing decisions, periodically check it against gross margin and understand the relationship between the two calculations.

A big part of becoming a successful ecommerce seller, and a fundamental lesson of Profit First, is learning to rely on numbers rather than feelings about how your company is performing.

Mark explained how he uses numbers to guide his decision-making. "I generally try to stay at a 30 percent margin for all my products. If it's under 30 percent, it really starts to not look super attractive," he said. "I have a couple products now that aren't costing me any money, but they're not making money. I could just keep them, and I might, but I also don't want to keep them if they're just there. They cost me some brain capacity. They cost my employee brain capacity. Maybe we could use that for something else. Also, I know that when you have something that's lower in profit, then it also takes more cash flow to be committed to that product. So it's just not as fun. So yeah, I try to stay at 30 percent."

Jeremy finds that another issue is tracking the cost of a product over time. He explains, "Each batch order of a product may have a unique price because of the quantity ordered or changing component costs, etc. In addition, Amazon may change their fees during the time your product is in their warehouse. Monitoring these numbers gives you the ability to adjust your pricing to maintain your margins. During your initial product evaluation, ensure that the market will allow you to price your product high enough to maintain adequate margins when price erosion occurs because of competition, Amazon fee changes, etc. Run scenarios for selling at X, Y and Z price points to ensure profitability at all levels."

Another gem of Robyn's is her advice to ensure the economics of one unit is considered at the time of sourcing. Here's how you do it. First, pick a month to analyze and calculate all of your fixed costs for that month. Next, look at how many total units you sold during the same month.

This is the P&L with fixed costs highlighted and averaged for the 8 months covered in the reporting period.

Profit and Loss
January - August, 2018

	Total
Income	1,428,626
Cost of Goods Sold	984,180
Gross Profit	444,447
Expenses	
Advertising/Promotion	97,767
Computer/Internet	97
Outside Services - Virtual Assistants	35,239
Product Liability Ins	9,069
Software Subscriptions	10,479
Bank Charges	724
Consulting Fees	3,000
Dues/Subscriptions	1,319
Insurance	1,635
Interest Expense	47
Legal/Professional Fees	8,198
Meals/Entertainment	590
Office Expenses	888
Payroll	36,000
Telephone Expenses	109
Training/Education	753
Travel	14,676
Exchange Loss / (Gain)	2,036
Total Expenses	221,148
Net Income	223,299

200,681	Total Fixed Expenses
25,085	Average for 8 Months
10,112	Average Orders for 8 months from Amazon Report, see example

2.5 Economics of One Unit

Every order has to result in a sale price of 2.5 time
the purchase to break evern

An order of a product that costs $7 must sell for more
than $7 * 2.5= $17.50 to breakeven

Next, divide the total fixed costs by the total units sold. To get this report from Seller Central at Amazon, select Reports>Fulfillment>All Orders, select Download tab> Order Date and your date range. For this example, I looked at All Orders for the same eight months of the P&L, January—August. If you have a large number of orders each month, I suggest running the report a month at a time and then averaging them. Once you download the report, filter the spreadsheet by **item-status** (column N), selecting only items shipped. Then use the autosum function to total all shipped units in the quantity column (column O). This will give you the value that each unit sold can contribute to cover your fixed operating expenses.

amazon-	merchar	purchase		asin	item-status	quantity	
	Data hidden for privac					9787	

When you evaluate your ROI, make sure that the profit component is large enough to more than cover the economics of one-unit value. Look at two or three months to see how this number varies. Then select the value that will ensure you will be covering your fixed costs when you apply it against the product's estimated ROI.

Sourcing using your ROI and the economics of one unit can help you make good inventory purchasing decisions. But there's one other area that you must monitor to ensure you are buying inventory that actually sells and doesn't just sit on a shelf at Amazon's warehouse. Robyn advises her clients to monitor their total inventory at Amazon over ninety days as a percentage of total inventory value. If this number stays at the same percentage or is growing, you are not scaling correctly. Your buying decisions should be moving toward quicker inventory turns. Watch this number every month to ensure your cash flow is not stuck in stale inventory.

To get this number, pull the Inventory Age report from Seller Central. Within Seller Central, select the following tabs: Fulfillment>Inventory> (show more)>Inventory Age. Add a column and insert your product costs for each SKU. Add a column to calculate the value of inventory on hand (multiply product costs times available quantities). Add another column to calculate the value of inventory over ninety days (multiply product costs times the quantities of products in the columns 91 to 180 days, 181 to 270 days, 271 to 365 days, and 365-plus days. See the partial report that follows. Note that the value of inventory over ninety days is $2461 and the total inventory value is $3178. To get your percentage of inventory that is over ninety days old, divide the value of the inventory over ninety days old by the total inventory value ($2461/3178 = 77%).

snapshot-date	Product Cost (added column)	fnsku	asin	product-name	condition	avaliable-quantity (sellable)	qty-with-removals-in-progress	Total Inventory Value (added column) C*(H-I)	inv-age-0-to-90-days	inv-age-91-to-180-days	inv-age-181-to-270-days	inv-age-271-to-365-days	inv-age-365-plus-days	Value of Inventory over 90 Days (added column) C*(K+L+M+N)
8/31/2018	18.99	data removed for protect privacy		removed for protect privacy	New	60	0	1139.4	13	7	13	27	0	892.53
8/31/2018	2.5				New	1	0	2.5	1	0	0	0	3	0
8/31/2018	2.7				New	4	0	10.8	1	0	0	0	0	8.1
8/31/2018	2.5				New	1	0	2.5	1	0	0	0	0	0
8/31/2018	2.5				New	4	0	10	0	0	0	4	0	10
8/31/2018	3.5				New	106	0	371	1	0	17	88	0	367.5
8/31/2018	12.89				New	1	0	12.89	1	0	0	0	0	0
8/31/2018	0.89				New	731	0	650.59	1	4	7	719	0	649.7
8/31/2018	0.7				Used	1	0	0.7	0	0	0	0	1	0.7
8/31/2018	3.29				New	48	0	157.92	42	2	3	0	1	19.74
8/31/2018	18.99				New	22	0	417.78	3	4	15	0	0	360.81
8/31/2018	3.29				New	2	0	6.58	0	0	0	2	0	6.58
8/31/2018	3.29				New	3	0	9.87	0	0	0	0	3	9.87
8/31/2018	0.75				Used	1	0	0.75	0	0	0	0	1	0.75
8/31/2018	1.89				New	1	0	1.89	0	0	0	1	0	1.89
8/31/2018	2.89				New	1	0	2.89	1	0	0	0	0	0
8/31/2018	18.99				New	3	0	56.97	0	3	0	0	0	56.97
8/31/2018	5.89				New	2	0	11.78	0	0	0	0	2	11.78
8/31/2018	3.29				New	19	0	62.51	19	0	0	0	0	0
8/31/2018	5.89				New	3	0	17.67	0	0	0	0	3	17.67
8/31/2018	0.89				New	4	0	3.56	0	0	0	0	4	3.56
8/31/2018	4.29				New	1	0	4.29	0	0	0	0	1	4.29
8/31/2018	3.29				New	62	0	203.98	56	6	0	0	0	19.74
8/31/2018	9.49				New	2	0	18.98	0	0	1	0	1	18.98
Totals								3177.8	140	26	56	841	20	2461.16

Total Inventory At Amazon over 90 days Old = 2461/3178

77%

This example, shown as it displays from Amazon, illustrates inventory that is not moving; naturally, the seller is looking for ways to turn this stale inventory into cash. And such data becomes more meaningful when tracked over time. Week by week, a seller can determine if efforts to remove stale inventory are successful or if other approaches should be tested. This type of data should be recorded and monitored as part of your key performance indicators.

Using the economics of one unit helps you look at your business from a high level. It gives you a place to start. Mark recalls a consultation he had with a part-time COO. "We just did a one-time deep dive into my business, and one of the experiments we ran together was to take all of my overhead and apply that to my products. So, say my product has a 35 percent margin. He pointed out that with HR and all these other costs that aren't obvious in the reporting tools that I use, actually it is a 16 percent margin. Nobody ever talks about that. First of all, most people don't even know that. Even I didn't know that. That's when we started to run the numbers, and some of the products actually looked unprofitable. Those that look like they're barely above water, now once you factor in all the other overhead costs, they're below water. That was really interesting."

FUNDING YOUR INVENTORY BANK ACCOUNT

IF YOU HAVE BEEN IN business a while, you can get your inventory funding number from the cash flow spreadsheet we presented in the previous chapter. Since the monthly cash flow spreadsheet is for one month, evaluate that number against your COGS number on your P&L if you have access to that information in an accounting system. Many of our clients use other software applications that collect information from Amazon and also track product cost information. These can be useful data sources as well, but they are also what I call open systems. Open systems are not reconciled with a financial data source like your bank or credit card statement, so there are many opportunities for this information to be erroneous. Be sure to watch your inventory bank account for the first two or three months to ensure that you are adequately funding the account and that money is accumulating at the proper rate for your next inventory buy. Your inventory bank account will not lie. If you are under-allocating to this account, you will not have enough funds to make your next purchase. You will have to borrow from your operating account, use a credit card, or take a loan. If you are committed to Profit First, you want to work your business away from borrowing and toward self-funding.

Many sellers are looking for a way to grow quickly, and buying inventory seems to be the yellow brick road. However, using borrowed funds to grow inventory can create more problems than it solves.

THE DANGERS OF BORROWING FOR INVENTORY PURCHASES

SOMETIMES, SELLERS BELIEVE THEIR ONLY option is to borrow in order to purchase inventory. In fact, many of our new clients rely on loans and credit cards, particularly to bridge slow periods. They make the minimum payments, then get additional loans to buy more inventory. They use the proceeds from the sale of the inventory to fund their operating expenses. Many times, they do not pay themselves, but happily invest in new apps or training to run their businesses. This becomes a vicious circle that inevitably ends when the cash coming in is insufficient to service the credit card debt and no other loan sources are available.

One of my clients, based in Australia, was starting Profit First and concerned because he always paid his credit card with sales from a future payout. It was a gamble that the inventory would sell. On the day his credit card company decided to lower his credit limit by $75,000, he understood why the Profit First approach was so important. He had to rely on his existing sales to pay his credit card. He made drastic cuts in his operating expenses to ensure that he could pay off the credit card and start to build his war chest for future growth. The first few calls we had together were all about borrowing money to grow faster. After the credit reduction, he saw the benefit of setting the funds aside from what he sold in order to have the funds to pay for the next order.

Even if you continue to use credit cards for inventory purchases, make sure you can pay your credit cards with funds present in your inventory account at the time you order. Carole describes her process: "For inventory, my supplier requires payment by check. This makes it even more critical for me to have enough funds in my inventory account so that I can pay the invoices on time and not bounce checks or have to pull funds from other accounts. I pay my operating expenses with my credit card twice a month and pay whatever the current balance is on the 10th and the 25th."

Profit First has put Carole in control.

Do you have the profit margins to repay a loan and set aside funds to make your replenishment order? It's a tall order if you are also depending on the business to provide you with a paycheck.

Chris Potter from Amazon's 5 Star Seller Society explains the concerns related to using credit, particularly Amazon loans, very well. "The payback terms of an Amazon loan are significantly different than a line of credit, and different strategies should be used based on what type of loan you have. Amazon loans typically require you to pay back the entire amount in equal chunks over the term of the loan. This is very similar to a secured loan you'll receive from a bank (usually used for equipment).

"With a line of credit, you usually only have to pay the interest each month, and you can pay it down as your business dictates. For planning purposes, you can somewhat expect the line of credit money will always be there. Due to this, you can plan to reorder items as necessary, and can effectively add the full line of credit to your inventory purchasing budget.

"For an Amazon loan, due to the quick repayment, it makes it difficult to reorder anything that sells through if you want to ensure the loan is fully paid off when due. Amazon loans tend to work best for scenarios where you need to buy a large quantity of a product at one time and will sell through the inventory as the loan needs to be paid off. This is perfect for one-time large liquidation buys or discontinued items. For regular, replenishable items, Amazon loans are not exactly ideal, because you can't always guarantee you'll have the cash to reorder when you are low.

"Too many people who take out Amazon loans spend all the money up front and then keep attempting to spend money on more product or reorders, as if the money will always be there. This ends up being a trap in which they struggle to have enough cash to pay off the Amazon loan. Near the end, in a lot of cases, it's almost necessary to take out a new Amazon loan (assuming one is offered again) to stay afloat. They are effectively treating an Amazon loan like it's a line of credit, when, in fact, the terms are quite different.

"Any way you look at it, if you are preparing to take on debt, make sure you have a specific plan for the type of debt you are taking on and execute that plan properly."

Chris Potter isn't saying there's no room in a profitable business model for borrowing money. He is saying that money should be borrowed wisely and managed carefully if you want to avoid being overwhelmed by debt.

Jeremy described the stress he's seen when friends have used loans: "I've had friends who have gone that route. They get caught in a trap, and there's nothing left at the end of the day. In fact, they're behind. It's an ugly cycle. The downfall of scaling. They plan to scale up as fast as possible, launch a bunch of products, and cash out as a millionaire. It doesn't always play out like people hope.

"It's interesting, because you have the added bonus of peer pressure, where you think, 'This guy has $1 million dollars in sales, now he's at $1.5 million, now he's at $5 million. Yeah, I'm gonna do that too!' But it comes with a big price. You have to make sure you're prepared. You borrow money now. Let's say you put out $100,000 to buy inventory because you took out a loan, but again, in the Amazon game, what's your real profit margin? Like 20-22 percent, 25 maybe, pre-tax? At that point, you're going to have to place a reorder before you've actually recouped any costs. You're that much farther from turning a real profit."

Not only can inventory bought with borrowed funds eat away at your profits, it can also eat away at your motivation and self-esteem. Debt is stressful.

INVENTORY THE PROFIT FIRST WAY

IN BUSINESS, AS IN LIFE, things rarely go as planned. That's why, in addition to setting aside funds to replenish stock, our clients build their inventory accounts to plan for the unexpected, such as Amazon losing inventory. Carole explains that ecommerce sellers should plan on dealing with missing inventory from time to time. She elaborates: "Amazon has probably lost everybody's inventory at some point. If they admit it, they will eventually refund you for it. In the meantime, you've got to scramble to get new inventory produced, and shipped. It's really helpful to have some money in the bank for inventory for these kinds of unexpected things."

In addition to having extra cash in the bank account to allow her to make another purchase, Carole made some other changes to minimize the risk of lost inventory. "I changed to only shipping one SKU, and not shipping combined SKUs, because it's a lot harder for Amazon to misplace your inventory into the wrong SKU if the box only contains one thing," she explained. "I'd rather send in smaller quantities frequently, because that way if there is a problem, it's on a smaller scale. The other good reason to ship small is that Amazon is increasing their storage charges. They want to discourage somebody shipping in a year's worth of product."

When you combine a sound inventory replenishment strategy with thoughtful, effective purchasing and shipping decisions, you're on the path to profitability.

Earlier, we learned that managing inventory is Mark's biggest challenge. After two and a half years of implementing Profit First, he has a new strategy. Mark said, "So now I have some cash flow to help me when I'm in a cash crunch. Actually, right now is a good example. We placed an order for my top seven or eight products to have three months' buffer inventory in a warehouse in China. And that inventory will be there to smooth out sales spikes I can't predict. Or maybe I can start doing lightning deals on Amazon.

"The important thing is, that buffer gives me options, because for me, being out of stock is a horrible feeling. It's like you lose money and you lose rankings. There are so many things you have to do to get back to where you were. That is very expensive. To create this buffer, I think we placed an order of around $60,000, and I only paid 30 percent down. It was an unexpected expense, and I had enough money in my accounts. In this case, it was an account we called the vault, which was just extra money to use to grow the business."

Mark now understands just how critical it can be to have cash reserves, rather than having to borrow huge sums of money to buy inventory. He mentioned "the vault." As you read further, you'll learn how and why to set up a vault of your own.

TAKE ACTION

KNOW YOUR NUMBERS! COMPARE THE ROI on your products to the gross margins on your P&L. Are they similar? If not, what is causing the difference?

Calculate the economics of one unit and begin using that as another data point in your purchasing decisions.

CHAPTER FOUR

The Foundational Profit First Bank Accounts for Ecommerce Businesses

SETTING UP BANK ACCOUNTS IN the US is usually a hassle. Many times, it requires an actual trip to the bank and having to produce an operating agreement for one's business. I remember spending an afternoon at my bank setting up these bank accounts and signing form after form. I also remember haggling with them over the fees.

My attempt at Profit First using ledger accounts on my books had failed. As Mike Michalowicz predicted, I continued to rely on my bank balance, as it was always up to date while my QuickBooks account was always a few days behind. And, just as Parkinson's Law states, I managed to use up the resources that were available in those accounts. I'm human too, and I wanted to escape the trap of always spending up to the balance in my accounts. I also wanted to test the Profit First system before I promoted it to my clients. So I opened the bank accounts.

Starting that first month, my business was profitable. I was stoked to see money growing in my Profit Account each month. I was also excited to have funds set aside for taxes when April arrived. Watching these accounts grow reenergized me and my business and gave me the real-world experience to help my clients.

I know the idea of spending an afternoon at the bank is not appealing. Let me assure you that it will be worth it. Really, the bank does all the work; you just have to sign the documents. When you have your accounts in place and are running your business on Profit First, you have a "done for you" cash flow dashboard. You will be able to manage your day to day business by looking at your bank accounts.

Carole told me, "I like the logic of having the different bank accounts and being able to really determine what percentage of my income I want to allocate to the different categories. I can balance inventory versus marketing and other expenses and still be able to put something away for profit and for owner's pay. Before we worked together on Profit First, I hadn't been pulling a specific amount for owner's pay. I think a lot of other people are in that situation too."

For Mark, the small plates approach to handling business revenue makes perfect sense and even informs his inventory strategy, which I mentioned in the last chapter. He said, "The inventory strategy, for example. Let's just say that I had one big bank account, and I can tell you right now, at this moment, there's probably about $200,000 in all my accounts together. Wild guess, but pretty close.

"If I had that amount of money in just one bank account, I would have no way of knowing if I had money to invest in a big inventory buy. Even though I can look at the account and say 'Wow, there's a lot of money in there,' I don't know what it's going to go for. Let's just spend it on something. That seems super careless to me. In this case, I can make that inventory investment knowing that that money isn't earmarked for something else.

Would I have made the same decision if I weren't doing Profit First? I don't know whether I would have or not. But now I know exactly what that decision means to me and the cash flow for all my other accounts."

After two and a half years, Mark has learned to trust our process. He said, "In general, my accounts seem to have more cash in them than I think they necessarily need, but I also know now, after being in this business for four years, that I'm going to need that money later on down the road. So I don't even look at it like extra money. It's just money saved up for when I need it later this year. For example, I have a new shipper. They seem to take forever to invoice me, and I really don't know how much I owe for shipping for all the purchase orders I've placed with them. I really don't know. I don't have any idea. And so, while my shipping account seems to have quite a bit of money, maybe $30,000 or so, I know that pretty much whatever they throw at me, I'm going to be able to handle."

I like to give our clients peace of mind around their finances. I love to hear Mark say, "I'm going to be able to handle it!"

Jeremy was wired for Profit First when he first came to me. He was already doing something similar for his personal bank accounts. He explained, "I was a sub account geek. I had a lot of sub accounts and I just never had thought to apply that to anything but my personal life. And then I read *Profit First*. And I was like, 'Oh, how have I been missing this my entire life on the business side?' It all just kind of clicked when we first talked. Geez, like, 'Yes, this is what I've been missing!'

"The value for me is when I log onto the bank account and I have the buckets in front of me. I feel comfortable about how the business is performing. Or uncomfortable, and then I know

I need to adjust because I better figure out what's going on here. It allows you to make a decision, which I think is important because the one bucket, it's too big, too vague. Am I going to make payroll this week? Or this month?"

It's easy to see the common threads running through Carole, Mark, and Jeremy's Profit First experiences. They relish knowing they've set aside enough money to cover expenses—even unexpected ones. And they love knowing their decisions are based on good data, a genuine sense of how their companies are doing.

Bank accounts designated for specific purposes are the key to making those good decisions for your business and to knowing how your company is doing. The basic Profit First accounts and an inventory account work well for most ecommerce businesses. How we handle the allocations between accounts can be unique in the ecommerce world. The main variations center around Amazon's biweekly payout structure net of fees and the use of an inventory account. There are also some advanced accounts that we've found useful that we will discuss in the next chapter. Let's dive in to how to use these bank accounts in our ecommerce world, starting with a fun account: income.

INCOME ACCOUNT

Do you need an income account? For ecommerce businesses with more than 80 percent of income from Amazon, taking a biweekly payout, you do not need a separate income bank account. In effect, Amazon is the bulk of your income and they are holding your funds for two weeks. This serves the purpose of an income account as described in *Profit First*: "When money comes into your main INCOME account, it simply acts as a serving tray for the other accounts. You then periodically disperse all the money from the INCOME account into different accounts in predetermined percentages."

Continue to have your Amazon deposit made into your operating expense account and make the transfers from this account.

If you have many selling platforms and you are getting payouts from them on different schedules, and the income from these channels is more than 20 percent of your income, then you should open an income account and follow a typical 10th and 25th rhythm for disbursing the funds as recommended in *Profit First*.

Carole shared a useful tip: "If anybody's thinking about changing their bank account that they have associated with their Amazon seller account, it's really, really important to give Amazon a heads-up, and let them know that you're going to be changing banks. I know of people who have gone into their seller account, changed the bank they were using, or changed their bank account number, and their account was immediately shut down because Amazon thought the change might be fraudulent. It's too important, so be careful if you're making this change."

Whether you simply use Amazon to hold and disburse your income or you set up a separate income account, that's your first step toward real profitability!

INVENTORY ACCOUNT

THE NEXT ACCOUNT WE WILL discuss is the inventory account. Profit First allocations are typically made from real revenue. Real revenue assumes that all your materials and subcontractors have been paid. For ecommerce sellers, we also have to ensure that we are setting funds aside for inventory. The best way to accomplish this is with a bank account. As discussed earlier, use the monthly cash flow spreadsheet to determine the amount that should be set aside to fund your inventory account.

When you go to fund your next inventory buy, you will have the funds set aside and you will not have to rely on borrowed funds. By designating an account for inventory, you will be able to clearly see the funds committed for this purpose. When you commingle your inventory and operating expenses, you can fall victim to Parkinson's Law. If you are operating with one checking account, it is too tempting for the cash building up in that account to be used for other purposes and it may not be there for the next inventory purchase.

Many ecommerce sellers like to use their credit cards to build up points for travel or other rebate programs. There are genuine benefits to using credit cards, like big cash-back rewards and fraud protection. While Profit First does not espouse credit card use, we do see how it can work for ecommerce sellers. One strategy is to have a separate credit card or cards designated for inventory. With this combination of designated inventory cards and account, you can monitor your inventory spending and ensure that there are funds in the inventory bank account to cover the balance on the credit card.

If you don't do anything else in this book, separate your inventory and your operating expense accounts and you will learn something powerful about your business.

While I was interviewing Jeremy for this book, he shared an anecdote. He said, "As we're sitting here, I just got invoices from one of the manufacturers. I'm looking and I have my bank account open on the other side; I see the invoice amount and

I'm like, 'Oh, geez.' I look at the little bucket and I'm like, 'Oh wait, we're good!' When we have Profit First dialed in, that's what you get—'We're good!'"

PROFIT ACCOUNT

THE PRIMACY EFFECT

The second behavioral principle you need to understand about yourself is called the Primacy Effect. The principle is this: we place additional significance on whatever we encounter first.

When we follow the conventional formula of **Sales – Expenses = Profit**, we are primed to focus on those first two words, *Sales* and *Expenses*, and treat *Profit* as an afterthought. We then behave accordingly. We sell as hard as we can, then use the money we collect to pay expenses. We stay stuck in the cycle of selling to pay bills, over and over again, wondering why we never see any profit.

When profit comes first, it is the focus, and it is never forgotten.

At this point you should have your existing checking account, which we will call your operating expense account, and an inventory account.

If your cash flow has been tight, add one more account for your initial setup. This is your profit account. This will be a savings account and we will begin by transferring 1 percent into the account with each payout. Be sure to watch your operating expense checking account as you transfer funds into the inventory checking and profit savings accounts. If you have been living off the float for inventory payments, it will no longer be available. ("Float" in this case is cash available to you that will be needed to replenish your inventory.)

You may run short on inventory or operating expense funds, or both. If this occurs, you know you have been living on borrowed funds to make things work, an all-too-common realization. It means you must get serious about ensuring that you make adequate gross margins and that your operating expenses are reduced. After your first quarter or two, begin to increase your profit percentage by 1 to 2 percent each quarter. You want to get up to between 5 and 20 percent, depending on the size of your business. Refer to the chart below and you can see your target percentage. Remember to select the column based on your real revenue, which is your top line revenue less your inventory and other cost of sales items like fees and prep centers, etc.

	A	B	C	D	E	F
Real Revenue Range	$0 - $250k	$250k - $500k	$500k - $1m	$1m - $5m	$5m - $10m	$10m - $50m
Real Revenue	100%	100%	100%	100%	100%	100%
Profit	5%	10%	15%	10%	15%	20%
Owner's Pay	50%	35%	20%	10%	5%	0%
Tax	15%	15%	15%	15%	15%	15%
Operating Expenses	30%	40%	50%	65%	65%	65%

You have mastered the inventory, operating expense, and profit accounts. You understand how the transfers work, and you're confident your percentages are right. Now let's take a bold step and add two more accounts. Typically, at this point, the business is showing an accounting profit. If that's the case, you should be paying your most important employee (YOU) and setting aside funds for the IRS bill that will inevitably arrive. It's time to open up two new accounts: an owner's pay checking account and a tax savings account.

OWNER'S PAY ACCOUNT

FOR THE OWNER'S PAY ACCOUNT, you may have to start small, like 5 percent. This is a great place to start! Remember, many small business owners never pay themselves. Try to match up the percentages for owner pay and taxes and implement them together. You will need to build up the tax account to approximately 15 percent (more on this account later), and owner's pay will be between 5 and 50 percent. (See the above chart in the previous section on profit accounts.) As the cash health of your business improves, you will take more for yourself in compensation for all your hard work.

Carole told me that she is aware of a lot of ecommerce business owners who are solopreneurs, so they don't have payroll set up, and there's no automatic amount being pulled and sent into their own personal checking accounts every month. She elaborates: "Having an allocated amount that I could take for owner's pay really helped me to see how well I was supporting myself with my business."

One question I am often asked is, "Why can't I just move my pay into my personal checking account?" People new to Profit First don't always get the purpose of an owner's pay account right off the bat. The allocation of funds to the owner's pay account is calculated as a percentage of your income. I suspect this amount varies, as you have months where sales fall behind and other months where they are stronger. You want that owner's pay account to weather the ebb and flow of your sales and provide you with a steady amount as a paycheck. Determine what amount you need to support your personal lifestyle on a monthly basis. Use half of that number as your goal amount to take from your business each payout. You may have to start at much less than that amount, and that is fine. Get started anyway, and make it a priority to move that number up each quarter. As you get a handle on your product margins and your cash flow, you will see how to make your steady paycheck.

During boom times, the owner's pay account will grow rapidly. During slow times, it will grow at a more modest rate. The objective is to build that account up so that it provides you with a steady paycheck and also a three to six-month reserve. Once you achieve this level in your owner's pay account, you and your family will be able to breathe easier when the unexpected happens in your business.

TAX ACCOUNT

FOR A VARIETY OF REASONS, this kind of account is often the least understood. There are several types of taxes at the state and federal level. The tax account is designated only for the business's income tax, both state and federal. It is not for sales tax, franchise tax, property tax, or payroll taxes, which, if significant, can be set aside in a separate account (more commonly, they are paid out of the operating expense account). The 15 percent target allocation may be confusing because it doesn't match the tax rates. This percentage is based on real revenue and, through Mike's research with thousands of businesses, it is adequate to cover a company's income tax bill. Note: this percentage does not change with the size of the business.

Another point of confusion arises from different business structures that have different tax payment options. Sole proprietorships and LLCs are considered disregarded entities, and taxes are filed on a schedule of the business owner's 1040 federal tax return and the personal state tax return. Taxes for an LLC or sole proprietorship are paid from the tax account. If there is not enough money, the owner must either reduce her compensation or take the money from the operating expense account. The profit account should never be touched.

If the business structure is an LLC with an S corp election, an S corporation, or a C corporation, the owner may be paid through payroll. In some cases, such as an LLC with an S election or an S corporation, the owner is required by the IRS to take a "reasonable" salary. In these businesses with a corporation structure, taxes are withheld from the owner's paycheck and therefore the owner pay account. The tax account is then used to reimburse the owner for the taxes.

Many of my clients struggle with the tax account. Withholding at 15 percent when their business is barely profitable ties up cash, even though the tax obligation is likely to be minimal. It's also difficult to forecast sales for the busy months. You may go three quarters operating at a loss and make that up in the fourth quarter, finishing the year with a large profit and a subsequent tax bill. Having your books in order helps you understand and prepare for these trends. A good relationship with your tax preparer is also extremely important to adequately plan for your taxes.

Visit your tax preparer at least twice per year. Of course, you will be talking in March or April, but consult with them in August or September, too. At that point, you will have several months' worth of historical data, which you can use to forecast your remaining months and get a range of the tax anticipated. With this information, you can adjust your tax account allocation during those remaining months if necessary. If Q4 is your busy time, you don't want to be tax planning in Q4. You will be too busy. You will also have more cash during this time, and will need to set it aside for your taxes. If it stays in your operating account, it is likely to get spent because Parkinson's Law will be in play.

Jeremy explained why he was his CPA's favorite client: "The first year of Profit First, my accountant didn't want to tell me how much I owed because he was afraid. Earlier in the day, the accountant had told another client what he owed in taxes and the client was upset and fired back, 'No way. I'm done!' Then he talks to me, and I'm like, 'Dude, just give me the number.' It was a big number, but I had it covered. I mean, it's all relative. I just moved the money out of my tax bucket into my checking accounts and was good to go. The accountant was just beating around the bush trying to make it a soft landing. I told him not to worry about it. It was all good."

OPERATING EXPENSES ACCOUNT

YOUR OPERATING EXPENSES ACCOUNT IS the account that will require your constant attention. Historically, you most likely used this account for all your transactions. Now you understand that we need to separate out inventory and profit from the start, and that owner's pay and taxes will also be pulled out when you get the system fully in play. That leaves you with the overhead portion of your business. This is where cash can be sucked right out of your business, leaving you to see no return on your investment.

I have noticed a common weakness for training, education, and SaaS apps amongst ecommerce sellers. Your chart of accounts in your accounting system should help you identify these expenses in a category called "software subscriptions" and give you a way to track what you're spending. It is exciting to learn a new technique that will be the next big thing, or, if you're a tech geek, to play with the latest software. However, that is not the way to grow your business. Focus and optimization are the keys to growth. A clear focus on your business will enable you to find ways to innovate and become more efficient. It is hard to see those patterns if you're distracted. It takes a deep dive to understand how your processes can be improved or how you may be able to negotiate better pricing on your products or shipping. If you're not looking at these areas closely, your competitor is. That competitor is optimizing while you are playing with the next shiny object.

Jeremy explained the importance of innovation: "Especially in the Amazon game, you need to continuously have a pipeline of products that you've been researching with the goal of launching. You have to launch more products. Because I think in the Amazon world, it's like a moth to a flame. With software like Jungle Scout, other sellers do research, see that there's a particular product having success, and then you find yourself with people hot on your tail, doing very, very similar things that appeal to your customers and steal your sales."

If you're investing all your time and expense money in sparkly new apps and unnecessary techniques, then you're not going to be able to stay ahead of the competition.

To keep these expenses in check, review monthly recurring expenses on a quarterly basis. Are you still using the software? Did the trial period run out, and is your credit card still being billed? Rigorously review software subscriptions and other like expenses quarterly and cut the dead wood.

Likewise, it's important that you examine your marketing expenses. Are you really getting a satisfactory return on your investment? It is tough to get attention for your products, but you can measure the results of your advertising campaigns. Keep an eye on them. A quick review of my clients who sell over $1 million a year shows an average investment of 6 percent in advertising, primarily made up of Facebook ads, Google ads and Amazon PPC. This is an anecdotal number, not based on industry research, but my clients are always looking for a comparison to help them understand their performance.

If you are using credit cards, be sure that you have a card designated for operating expenses. As you allocate your income, you can assess the amount set aside for operating expenses against the charges you have accumulated on your credit card. Pay off that credit card balance each time you make your allocations so that it stays in check. If you are carrying a balance, then you are spending more than your business can support. Get back in control and cut out the unnecessary expenses.

You may have to innovate and look for new ways to be efficient. One of my favorite strategies is to just delay. Mike tells a story in his book about simply telling yourself, "I'll go to the store and buy that tomorrow." As I have employed that strategy in my own life, I have learned just how many of my purchases were impulse buys. After I've put off the purchase for a few days and that sense of urgency has passed, I find I can more clearly evaluate the need. Sometime, the need is real; many times, it's just a want.

A different strategy for managing operating expenses is needed during your high sales season. As we have discussed, you will be using an allocation percentage of your sales to fund your operating expense account. Remember, when we did the monthly cash flow spreadsheet in Chapter Two, we deliberately used a normal month so your allocation percentage will cover your expenses based on normal sales. During your busy season, your operating expenses don't typically change that much compared to the rest of the year. We still have the same rent and software subscriptions, insurance etc. However, your income does change. Consequently, we find that using the same allocation percentages funds all of our accounts with a higher dollar amount. In other words, you will have more money flowing into your operating expense account than you need to operate the business.

If you don't have a strategy to handle higher sales income and subsequently higher allocations to your operating expense account, Parkinson's Law will creep in and before you know it, your operating expenses will sneak up to meet the new cash level in the account. Don't wait until your busy season to do these calculations and make the necessary changes. Work ahead!

The general strategy is to look at your typical monthly expenses and have that number in mind as your desired cash balance in your operating expense bank account. It's easy to get this amount if you run your profit and loss report year-to-date by month. Scan your operating expenses totals and pick the value that will ensure you will have the cash flow to cover your expenses during the busy season. You may want to even give yourself 10-15 percent extra as a cushion. Then, each time you make your allocations, look at the current balance in the account and subtract it from the desired balance for the account. The resulting difference is the dollar amount you want to move into your operating expense account, if you are depositing your payout into an income account. If you are depositing your payouts directly into your operating expense account, then after you transfer your allocations out for all the other accounts, compare the current account balance with the desired account balance. Any amount left in the income account or over the desired account balance should be transferred to your profit account (or a drip account that we will discuss in the next chapter). In January, when the dust settles, we can determine the best use for those funds.

In the example that follows, the most recent four months, May—August, show average expenses of $5,941 per month. Knowing that business is going to pick up for the rest of the year, I would recommend using the $7500 as the cash balance level to be maintained. This is a little higher than July, which was an outlier month in terms of expenses.

PROFIT AND LOSS
January - August, 2018

	JAN 2018	FEB 2018	MAR 2018	APR 2018	MAY 2018	JUN 2018	JUL 2018	AUG 2018	TOTAL
Income									
▸ AMZ Product Charges	10,049.44	7,869.95	9,728.27	11,805.67	17,485.07	29,474.90	29,647.74	22,930.79	$138,991.83
AMZ Vendor Express Sales	194.00	129.00	78.00	165.00	295.00	293.00	196.00		$1,350.00
▸ Paypal Product Sales	697.57	391.32	493.93	557.68	531.16	483.29	419.83	300.49	$3,875.27
▸ Shopify Income	1,073.36	577.52	744.35	804.05	1,077.32	731.88	661.67	1,152.98	$6,823.13
Total Income	$12,014.37	$8,967.79	$11,044.55	$13,332.40	$19,388.55	$30,983.07	$30,925.24	$24,384.26	$151,040.23
▸ Cost of Goods Sold	$7,442.17	$5,819.05	$5,622.04	$8,448.21	$11,770.81	$22,179.79	$22,196.97	$16,278.66	$99,757.70
GROSS PROFIT	$4,572.20	$3,148.74	$5,422.51	$4,884.19	$7,617.74	$8,803.28	$8,728.27	$8,105.60	$51,282.53
▾ Expenses									
Bank Charges			99.00						$99.00
Insurance					2,250.00				$2,250.00
▸ Marketing Expenses	1,471.93	2,366.15	1,489.05	2,232.12	1,693.92	6,380.52	6,886.40	4,195.12	$26,715.21
Meals	8.82				95.58				$104.40
Office Expenses	27.97		18.12						$46.09
Office Expenses & Supplies				6.50	81.25	32.41			$120.16
Other Miscellaneous Expense	193.90								$193.90
Phone Service	31.02	17.84	18.14	22.73	19.84	19.67	21.33	20.55	$171.12
Product development				11.09					$11.09
Professional Services	303.00	303.00	768.00	303.00	303.00	303.00	303.00	303.00	$2,889.00
Training and Conferences		10.65		75.00	699.00				$784.65
Travel	278.00		258.59		40.47			117.98	$695.04
Total Expenses	$2,314.64	$2,697.64	$2,650.90	$2,650.44	$5,183.06	$6,735.60	$7,210.73	$4,636.65	$34,079.66
NET OPERATING INCOME	$2,257.56	$451.10	$2,771.61	$2,233.75	$2,434.68	$2,067.68	$1,517.54	$3,468.95	$17,202.87
▸ Other Income	$0.59	$0.50	$0.36	$0.34	$0.41	$0.28	$0.27	$0.27	$3.02
▸ Other Expenses	$550.27	$59.15	$58.97	$58.98	$73.96	$14.99	$29.98	$14.99	$861.29
NET OTHER INCOME	$-549.68	$-58.65	$-58.61	$-58.64	$-73.55	$-14.71	$-29.71	$-14.72	$-858.27
NET INCOME	$1,707.88	$392.45	$2,713.00	$2,175.11	$2,361.13	$2,052.97	$1,487.83	$3,454.23	$16,344.60

This is such a critical component of Profit First that I'm going to repeat this process from another perspective: The order of operations matters when it comes to distributing money among your small plates. That means you take the deposit from Amazon, move funds based on your normal allocation percentages to your inventory account, then your profit account, then owner's pay and taxes. The remaining amount is available for your operating expense account. At this point, do the comparison described above. Any amount over the desired level of your operating expense account should be moved out to your profit account or a drip savings account.

The drip savings account is an advanced Profit First account, and in Chapter Five, I will explain how to use this account. Your busy season is not the time to spend that money. You are too busy to think clearly about the best use for those funds. Leaving excess dollars in operating expenses will set you up to be a victim of Parkinson's Law. Take an extra minute and move the cash to a special account so you will not be tempted.

Carole's Emu Joy health and beauty product line always had steady sales without much seasonal impact. Last summer, she introduced a product to treat bug bites, and suddenly she had a hot-selling item during the summer months. Her revenues were great last summer, and as I did her quarterly review of her Profit First accounts in September I could see the impact of her increased revenue and how that increased funding in her operating expense account. And just as Mr. Parkinson predicted, her operating expenses increased accordingly. We discussed this strategy of a static funding level versus an allocation percentage, and Carole is excited to put the static funding level strategy in place for the upcoming bug bite season, aka summer.

Now we've covered the basic Profit First accounts and how they can work for you. Once again, the best advocate for the system is a client who's made it work. Mark sums up the power of Profit First nicely: "By allocating my payout every two weeks, I get a good sense of where the business stands. I realize there's probably nothing dramatic that's going to happen in the next two weeks that's going to rock my boat too hard. And at this point, I've been working this way for a while. So even when an account has more than I think it needs, like for instance a marketing account, I know it's the right thing to do.

"Like we talked about, my associates in this business would tell me I'm crazy. They think I should be spending that money to build my business. But I just feel very, very comfortable knowing that if some random invoice comes from some shipping company that I hadn't thought about, I got it covered. And that makes me feel really stoked. I have to admit I didn't really get it when we first started working together. Until you start putting your money in separate accounts, seeing where your cash flow goes, you really don't get the power of it."

Profit First isn't magic, but it is powerful. It's a simple strategy that puts you in control of your company's revenue and encourages sound business decision-making.

One of my favorite things is finding out how my clients have made Profit First a part of their lives. For example, Jeremy dedicates Thursday to finances. "Every other Thursday, I go through the Profit First allocation process," he explained. "It's a couple minutes. A minute to put the number in and see what the buckets are, because I have my spreadsheet that does that for me. And then another couple minutes to transfer the money in. Which is fun because you get to see, 'Oh look! I have a couple more dollars in my profit account, let me get that next quarter.'"

Get your Profit First buckets ready, and watch them fill up!

TAKE ACTION

GET THOSE BANK ACCOUNTS SET up.

Make your first allocations following the percentages you calculated using the monthly cash flow spreadsheet.

CHAPTER FIVE

Advanced Accounts

Congratulations! You're now acquainted with the basics of Profit First specifically geared toward ecommerce sellers. You've learned how to divvy up your revenue into the basic buckets that will help you pay bills, pay yourself, turn a profit, and manage your all-important inventory. But, as you might guess, we're not going to just stop with the basics. You still have more to learn about managing your business profitably.

DRIP ACCOUNT

When you complete your profit assessment as described in Chapter Two, you typically review your business financials for a full year. The profit assessment is a great tool for understanding the overall health of your business. However, when your business cycle includes a peak season, you will manage your business differently for three quarters of the year, usually with much less income than during the boom quarter.

In order to take a conservative and functional approach to managing the business, we analyze and develop the allocation percentages based on the slower quarters, so that you can right-size your expenses for all twelve months. Then we develop a strategy for managing the additional funds coming in during the boom quarter. It's time to bring a special bank account into play, the drip account, which is funded with the proceeds from the boom quarter.

As described in Chapter Four, you will manage operating expenses based on a dollar level instead of a percentage allocation during your busy season. During that boom quarter, a percentage of a much larger amount can cause us to overinflate our operating expenses. You want to understand the monthly operating expenses needed. They don't typically vary that much month to month and are not significantly affected by seasonal sales.

Most of our ecommerce clients have seasonal fluctuations in their business, whether they have the typical Q4 holiday surge or rake in dollars from summer bikini sales, and the drip account is used to smooth out that seasonality. We often call the drip account our squirrel fund. We all know the squirrel working hard in the sweltering heat all summer long, building a nest and gathering nuts to store for the winter. When the winter weather arrives, the squirrel is warm and well fed. The squirrel was smart and prepared.

We want to be like the squirrel, but Mark explained that's something you learn the longer you're in business. "Seasonality is something that requires some maturity, too, because also it takes time to recognize and plan for variations. So now we're talking about three-year cycles to learn what seasonality means to you and your business.

"Before Profit First, in January, February, March, I would think, 'Oh my god, I'm rich. I'm rich. I'm just rich.' And it felt good. I had $100,000 in my bank, not knowing what was coming in June, July, August, the slow months. You better have money saved up for those months. Otherwise, you're dipping into your line of credit, and you're not feeling so good about where you're at."

Mark's drip account worked exactly like it was supposed to, providing funds during the lean times.

Jeremy explained how he monitors his accounts and makes changes. "I've adjusted the inventory bucket when I've noticed it was overfunded. I put a little more money into the drip account, and a little more into owner's pay. I saw we had a surplus 'cause we weren't doing as many product launches." At tax time, Jeremy uses some of his drip account to fund his SEP (Simplified Employee Pension) IRA and help minimize his tax burden. It's a good strategy to have cash available to invest in your retirement.

Because ecommerce businesses ebb and flow, it's important to save in prosperous times for your leaner months. This makes sense, so why is it so hard to do? Again, Parkinson's Law is at work. The solution is to use this special account to accrue funds for our slow months.

Here's how the drip account allocation works. We touched on this process in Chapter Four, as it all starts with managing your operating expense account. It is such an important facet of any business with seasonality, we will go over it again in this context.

During your peak season, manage your Profit First allocations as you normally would except for your operating expenses. Since your percentages were created based on a lower sales volume, you've been funding your operating expenses just fine at that lower sales volume. Typically, fixed-type operating expenses don't really increase during peak seasons. Rent stays the same, software expenses stay the same, and you pay yourself a consistent amount. During peak season, you would suddenly add as much as 5-20 times the needed amount into your operating expense account if you continued the allocation process with normal percentages. This would not be prudent; you likely have a way to invest those funds that would bring a greater return to your business than operating expenses. You could create a new percentage allocation scheme, but this is all happening when you're super busy! I developed this quick process to ensure you build up your drip savings account:

1. When you receive your Amazon payout, pay for the inventory you just sold. If you owe creditors for your inventory, set funds aside to take care of paying for these expenses first.

2. Next, calculate your average monthly operating expenses for the year. Let's say that you have average operating expenses of $5,000 each month. Ensure you have that amount in your bank account to cover your operating expenses until the next payout.

3. Pay yourself and set aside taxes using the normal Profit First allocation percentages—take care of you and your obligations.

4. Save! Move the remaining funds to a separate savings account—your drip account, or squirrel fund. If you do not have a drip account set up, move the money to your profit account. Do not leave it in your operating account. Out of sight, out of mind! As this account builds and you get past your busy season, you can slow down and think about how you might strategically use those funds.

Mark keeps a close eye on his operating expense account. "I try to keep around $15,000 to $20,000 in there, although I probably could take it lower than that," he told me. "And instead of adjusting the percentages when it gets up to $25,000 or $30,000,

I just move that extra $10,000 into the vault [more about that type of account below]. You'll be surprised how quickly your savings account accumulates."

Depending on your business needs and strategic plan, you could use these funds in a variety of ways. Try earmarking them for:

1. **Taxes.** We all dread tax season, but if you have been planning and saving, it makes tax time less stressful. Check in with your CPA early in January, especially if you've had a bigger Q4 than you anticipated. You may want to use some of these funds for tax purposes, either paying taxes or investing in a retirement-type savings plan.

2. **A cushion.** If you have savings, you can use these dollars to supplement your paycheck or operating expenses during your business off-season or when times are slow. If I know I'm going to be scaling and adding additional resources, I make sure that my drip account can be "metered" out over the time when I have expenses and before the investment starts to pay off.

3. **To grow your business.** Perhaps you're considering changing your business model. You can use your savings to switch from retail arbitrage to wholesale, or launch a new private label product. Maybe you consistently run out of inventory; these funds could allow you to build your inventory stock. As mentioned above, there is typically a period in which you make an investment and the payoff comes later. Use the drip account to help cover your expenses over that time period.

Another opportunity to fund your drip account comes from the biweekly nature of the Amazon payout program. If you are taking biweekly payouts, then you will be paid twenty-six payments during the year. Operating expenses are paid to vendors on a monthly basis. Rent, software, and other fixed expenses are all paid once a month. When you receive that third payment two times a year, do you have a plan for those funds? Set aside funds to cover your inventory and profit allocations, and then move the rest to your drip account. Remove the temptation—save yourself!!

Clients have found remarkable success by following our rule, "When in doubt, open an account!" In addition to the drip account, we have clients who have set up some combination of the following advanced accounts:

- Product development account. This account sets you up for growth on your terms, not the bank's. When you borrow money, you must pay those funds back on the bank's terms. Your revenue needs to be high enough to cover your replenishment costs, your operating expenses, and the interest and principal on the loan. Can you afford this? One way to know and to grow is to set aside funds to roll out a new product and become your own bank. This will give you the freedom to launch when you can afford it. Determine the amount you will require to launch your product, and see Chapter Seven, where we help you reverse engineer your product profitability.

- Shipping/freight account. Most of our clients include shipping and freight as part of their inventory account, along with prep center fees or any activity that adds value to their product and gets it to market. If you are shipping from China, either by air or boat, these expenses, along with bonding and custom agents, can add up to a significant cost. If you want to track shipping separately to ensure that you are setting aside adequate funds to pay for the next batch of inventory, create a separate account. Monitor your shipping costs as a percentage of the payout, using the same methods we discussed for the monthly cash flow spreadsheet. Then, when you make your allocations each payout, you will set aside the funds needed to get your next order to market.

- Advertising account. Like inventory, advertising takes up a large portion of your operating expenses. And advertisers are good at showing how an investment in advertising provides a great return. Monitor this closely. Evaluate and test how marketing drives your revenues. We recently worked with a client to monitor how an additional $200,000 in advertising over six months was impacting his sales. As you might expect, he did see a bump in revenue, but factored against the expense, the impact on the profitability of his business was negative. He has since dialed in his strategy and is setting up an account that will be used to fund advertising. In this way, he will see and track a direct connection between advertising dollars available in his bank account and the charges for advertising hitting his credit card. If this gets out of line, it will be obvious when he evaluates his weekly ad spend.

- Payroll account. If you have a team, it is likely that you worry about making payroll. As an entrepreneur myself,

I understand that responsibility. To ensure that you have funds available for this essential expense, determine your payroll as a percentage of your payout. With each payout, move the funds into the payroll account. To make this calculation, look at gross wages plus additional payroll taxes needed.

Biweekly payrolls will occur twenty-six times in a year, and if you are allocating based on Amazon's biweekly payout, this coincides well. However, if your payroll is biweekly and you are allocating funds twice a month on the 10th/25th schedule, remember to set aside enough money to cover the two extra payrolls each year. Calculate your normal biweekly payroll and multiply by 1/13. Add this amount to the normal biweekly amount; the total is the amount you should set aside in the payroll bank account. These extra funds will build up over the thirteen weeks, and then be available to fund that third payroll that occurs two months out of each year. It feels really good not to be scrambling for that extra payroll.

A common question I get from clients is, "Can I afford to hire another employee or to give raises?" To make that determination, and be prepared for the expense, increase your allocation in the payroll account for three months as a trial. Determine the cost of the additional staff member, or the cost of pay increases, and add it to the normal amount you allocate to the payroll account. This will reduce your operating expense allocation, so watch that account carefully. If you can manage for three months without having to borrow from this account for other purposes, then you are most likely able to afford the additional payroll expense.

- Sales/VAT tax account. I am writing this on the day the SCOTUS ruled that states can collect sales tax even if the seller doesn't have a nexus based on a physical location in the state. I'm sure that much will be sorted out by individual states by the time this is published, but the ruling will likely have a big impact on ecommerce sellers. It can be hard to come up with as much as 10 percent of your revenues, especially if you are only required to pay taxes annually. In addition to the tax itself, the cost of registering in each state is typically around $200. If you fund a sales tax account, be sure that you look at the percentage of total revenue, not just your payout. Since your payout is net of fees, and you are allocating on that basis, you can't just multiply an average sales tax rate by the payout. Since Amazon may reduce your payout by 30 percent or more, your sales tax allocation would be at least 30 percent short when it is time to make the tax payment. If you use a service like Tax Jar to automate this function, you can also use their reports to set aside the exact amount you will be liable to pay.

- Licensing/royalty/commission bank account. If you owe some portion of your revenue for a licensing fee or commission, set that money aside so you don't have to scramble to come up with it monthly or quarterly as required in your agreement. As with sales tax, understand that your commission terms may be based on units or revenue dollars for a particular item. Applying a percentage to your payout may not correlate directly, but you can make an educated estimate and adjust the percentage based on a few months of experience.

• Vault account.

The Vault is the place where you keep the cash saved to operate your business unscathed for three months if all sales came to a screeching halt and not another penny came into the business. The Vault account is an ultra-low-risk, interest-bearing account that you can use for short-term emergencies. At a certain point, leaving 50 percent in your PROFIT account to act as a rainy-day fund is not prudent because the money flow is a little unpredictable. A bad quarter won't contribute much to the PROFIT account. Then you take 50 percent out for a profit share, and now that PROFIT account reserve might be too small to sustain a big business. The question isn't whether you will have a dark day (your supplier goes out of business, your biggest client goes bankrupt, your best employees leave to start a direct competitor, and your clients decide to go with them, etc.). The question is, *when*? The Vault is there for that.

When you set up the Vault, you *must* also establish certain rules for its use. What I mean is that when you have a situation so dire that you need to access this money, you also have instructions written in advance on how to proceed. For example, if the money is pulled due to a drop in sales, you will preplan that besides just trying to get more sales, you will also cut all the related costs in your business within two months if things haven't improved. Few people have the discipline to think clearly or act appropriately in times of panic, and that's why we document a simple set of instructions for ourselves in advance.

The idea behind the Vault and the entire Profit First system is that it puts your decisions well out in front of any money crisis. Your business dynamics may not, in fact, improve; but your decision making will be much further out in front of the actual financial impact. So the goal of the Vault is *not* to buy time; it may afford some time to address unexpected challenges, but it is really about forcing important decisions early, so your business doesn't go into a cash crisis.

There is not much to add to Mike's original insight, because the vault works the same way in an ecommerce business. I will say that this is the account that will buy you freedom. Build it for a rainy-day fund; use it to invest in your business when an opportunity arises, or to invest in another business that builds diversity in your portfolio; put it to work launching a new product.

Carole has a great reason for building your vault account. "Everybody gets at least one product—if not their whole account—suspended by Amazon at some point," she told me. "It's not a matter of if; it's a matter of when. Literally every seller I know has had at least a product suspended, and usually for no good reason.

"The advantage of Profit First is that you do have that cushion in there to take care of your own living expenses or to make payroll. I've heard of people who have had their account suspended for something that they didn't do, or something that a black hat competitor did, and they've had to lay off their people. It's heartbreaking. People are losing their jobs because some competitor went and filed a false counterfeit claim, and

Amazon's reaction is to just shut down your account. Act first, and ask questions later.

"The thing is, if somebody had a Profit First system going, they would have that cushion sitting right there in their vault account that could hopefully tide them over until the situation got resolved, which can often take many weeks. Like I said, it's not a matter of if. It's a matter of when. Everybody gets shut down for all kinds of bizarre reasons. You can be doing everything right, play by the rules, be a squeaky-clean seller, and you can still get shut down. I got shut down because my product contained apricot oil, and Amazon suddenly thought it caused cancer. I had to convince them that wasn't true. They shut down another product of mine recently because I mentioned arthritis in the product description. They said I couldn't mention that, even though all the other competitive products mention arthritis.

"It takes a lot of time to fight this kind of thing. You have to go back and forth with written and phone conversations. A lot of people have to hire professionals for this. There are people who have a business built solely for helping people get reinstated. If you're shut down, your best option may be to spend several thousand dollars to hire a professional to help you."

If all your sales temporarily vanished, would you have the resources to keep the lights on? With a funded vault account, the answer would be yes.

Mark had another example where the vault account helped him. He said, "I had a potential patent lawsuit that ended up costing me $25,000 to settle. And I had the money. That's something you're just never going to be able to predict. And yeah, it's not fun to pay that bill even when you have money, but it's got to be worse when you don't." The vault can save your bacon and keep your business afloat.

Jeremy's rainy day happened when he realized he was losing sales because a competitor had infringed on his copyrights. In addition to lost revenue, he ended up spending many hours fighting the issue. He said, "We ended up taking down the competitor, because we bought their products, and they pretty much copied, word-for-word, almost all of our text in the actual book itself, which we have copyrights on. So we had to send a cease and desist letter, and they stopped that version and reconfigured and came out with similar but different version. That happens, I think, very frequently in the Amazon world and the business world in general. I know it's true for ourselves, as well as our friends and other colleagues who are doing different niches and different products. Everyone is facing a similar game. The number one challenge is making sure you are continually innovating and having products that you can bring to market that are differentiated from everybody else's."

If you have a drip or vault account, you can use those funds to supplement your owner pay or operating expenses when you lose sales. You can also accelerate a product launch if you need to get another product in play more quickly.

You may be thinking that the prospect of managing all these accounts sounds intimidating, but let's see how Mark, our power account-user, makes this all work. At last count, he had nine bank accounts. He explained, "It's not hard to manage. Most of those accounts are with one bank, so it's really easy. As soon as I get paid out from Amazon, I make the transfers from my operating account to my other eight accounts. And with my bank, each account can have a debit card attached to it. So, for my shipping account, I link all my shipping agent payment methods. The whole thing is easy. It never feels burdensome. I think it probably takes me twenty minutes or so every two weeks.

"Once I started to learn how Profit First worked, it was my call when to open a new account. I would add another account when I started to realize there was something unique about a category of expenses, and also when I realized they were going to be big enough where I had to really think about them. I mean, I still have tons of expenses that come directly out of my operating account, because they're tiny little expenses for staplers and stuff that I can pay just cash for. But when it becomes something that is a sizeable part of my business, it has to have its own account.

"I wouldn't think twice about it. I think with nine accounts, I've got myself pretty covered at this point, but I'd be open to opening twelve accounts, fifteen accounts, if it made sense. It doesn't feel like any burden to me at all."

Whether you're like Mark, who's comfortable sorting funds into many buckets, or you want to start with the minimum and see how it goes, Profit First's small plates mindset helps you prepare, both for challenges and for successes.

TAKE ACTION

EXAMINE YOUR EXPENSES AND CONSIDER your goals. What other accounts would help you keep track of cash as you manage your expenses and prepare to meet those goals? Set up those accounts at your bank.

CHAPTER SIX

Cash Flow: How to Manage Cash, and How to Keep it

ENFORCING A RHYTHM

Just as the rhythm of eating three meals a day keeps us from starving and bingeing on food, enforcing a rhythm works with money, too. When we get into a rhythm, we don't get into the reactive mode of crazy spending when we get big deposits and panicking in the face of big cash dips. I am not saying the money will automatically appear and you'll always have cash at your disposal, but establishing a rhythm will get you out of the daily panic. In fact, establishing a rhythm will also be a great indicator of overall cash flow. This system is the easiest way to measure cash flow. Instead of reading the cash flow statement (which, honestly, when was the last time you did that?), you can measure your cash flow by just checking your bank accounts, which you do anyway.

On a daily basis, I let the bills come in and I deposit income. I no longer do accounting when I have time or when someone calls to check to see if I received an invoice. I have a rhythm. I do my accounting every tenth and twenty-fifth (or the business day prior if the tenth or twenty-fifth fell on a weekend or holiday). This is the 10/25 Rule.

First, I tally all the new deposits from the last few weeks, and do the Profit First allocations, moving money into each account. Then I tally up all the bills and put them in the system.

By looking at my bills and my deposits two times a month, on the same days each time, I can see patterns.

When you get into a rhythm with your cash management you'll have your finger on the pulse of your business. You will monitor your cash position every day by just looking at your bank account. Log in. Spend two seconds looking at your balances. Log out. You will know where you stand that quickly. Think of your cash flow as waves rolling onto the beach. If the cash wave is big, you will notice and take action. When the waves are small, you will surely notice that, too. Most of the time, I expect the cash waves will be normal, and no action will be required. But no matter what, you will always know. Because you will continue to do what you normally do: log into your bank account.

Before I started managing my business with Profit First, I had no sense of how cash came and left my business. It was just random noise. If my bank account was large from a deposit, I started thinking of things I "needed." If it was small, I felt more pressure to give away services to close a sale, or I would slow down a project for my business so the payments I had to make would be delayed. This reactionary management of money was neither serving my peace of mind nor the health of my business. Enforcing a rhythm put me back in the driver's seat. While money is not always as plentiful as I'd like, it stays in that normal range most of the time. And I have a profit account that has my back!

Carole explained her process. "It literally takes me five minutes on the 10th and the 25th to do what I have to do. I open up my credit card statement. I see how much is due and check the current balance. Then I open up my bank account, and I make my transfers. It takes me two minutes to make all five of those transfers. Then I pay the credit card, and it's done. It's a five-minute exercise. I put it in my calendar so it automatically pops up on the 10th and 25th of every month, and nothing could be easier."

Rhythms and habits are powerful, and the most basic principle of Profit First is that we can create positive habits with long-term benefits. Mark's process is similar. "Amazon pays me out, and the very first thing I do is put all that money in all the accounts," he said. "The very second thing I do is I pay off my credit cards. And that way I know, okay, in this moment, I'm taken care of. All my operating accounts are in one bank. My profit account is in another bank. And I think that's the only external account that I have, so it's really easy."

As Mark explains, using the Profit First model really doesn't take any more time than you would typically spend to pay your business bills…it just has profit at the end of the rainbow.

Jeremy explains his two-week cadence: "Everything for me is just at one local credit union. I have six accounts: op. ex., owner's pay, tax, profit, inventory and drip. For me it's very manageable. It takes me a couple of minutes."

Step one for managing cash flow is redistributing your revenue into your buckets. There are two basic strategies for this allocation, depending on how often revenue is deposited into your income bank account. The two strategies are described in detail below.

ECOMMERCE SELLERS WITH REVENUE PREDOMINANTLY FROM AMAZON

CLIENTS THAT SELL ONLY ON Amazon or make more than 80 percent of their sales on Amazon typically have a biweekly payout rhythm imposed upon them. While this rhythm doesn't exactly fit the 10/25 rule Mike recommends, it is an effective way to manage your cash based on the payout cycle.

When you receive your biweekly payout, simply use the allocations developed from the cash flow spreadsheet to transfer your payout into the proper accounts.

This rhythm does have an added bonus. If Amazon disburses to you biweekly, they will actually disburse twenty-six payouts per year. Most months, you will receive two payouts; however, two months out of the year you will receive a third. Take a look at your payout schedule and mark those three-payout months on your calendar. We have plans for those months!

When you receive a third payout, fund your inventory, profit, owner's pay, and tax accounts as usual. But take the amount normally allocated to operating expenses and move it to your profit account or your drip account. This money will be used for something special. We don't want Mr. Parkinson's Law to take effect.

ECOMMERCE SELLERS WITH LOW AMAZON REVENUE

WHEN WEBSITE SALES OR OTHER channels make up more than 20 percent of your sales, or if you have an Amazon account that allows you to take more frequent payouts, you will want to follow the 10/25 rule. This is described in the box above and is the typical rhythm applied in most businesses. You will also want to add the income account to your bank accounts.

The income account—which should be a checking account—is your serving tray. All of your income will go into this account, and it will accumulate until the 10th and 25th of each month, the days on which you make your allocations.

The allocation process is the same as we have described before: transfer funds to your inventory account first, then to your profit account, owner's pay, taxes, and finally operating expenses.

In Chapter Four, we discussed how to manage the operating expense account during your high sales season. If your business is seasonal, you should employ that strategy during the season.

PROFIT DISTRIBUTION

NOW, THE FUN PART: TAKING your profit distribution! Let's get Mike's take on profit distributions:

PROFIT DISTRIBUTION

The profit distribution is an award to the equity owners (you and anyone who invested in the business with money or sweat) for having the courage and risk tolerance to start the business. Don't confuse the profit distribution with Owner's Comp, which is pay for working in the business. Profit is a reward for owning the business. Just as you get a profit distribution when you own shares in a public company, for which you didn't do squat workwise, so do you get a piece of the profit from your own company. Profit is a reward for equity owners, and Owner's Comp is the pay for people who are owner operators in the business.

The calendar quarters of every year are as follows:

Quarter 1—January 1 to March 31
Quarter 2—April 1 to June 30
Quarter 3—July 1 to September 30
Quarter 4—October 1 to December 31

On the first day of each new quarter (or the first business day afterward), you will take a profit distribution. Remember, the PROFIT account serves a few purposes:

1. Monetary reward for the equity owners of the business.
2. A metric to measure growth.
3. Cash reserve for emergencies.

Tally the total amount of profit in the account (don't add any quarterly distribution percentages from deposits you received this day, yet) and take 50 percent of the money as profit. The other 50 percent remains in the account, as a reserve.

Regardless of the day you start doing Profit First, take a distribution for the current quarter on the first day of the new quarter. For example, let's say you decide to implement Profit First on August twelfth. You allocate to your multiple accounts from that day forward. Then on October first, or the first day of the new quarter that you do your bookkeeping, you distribute the profit in the PROFIT Account. Whether you start this process on July third or September thirtieth, the next quarter still begins as of October first; so you distribute profits for the prior quarter that day. It doesn't matter when you start doing Profit First; what matters is that you get into a quarterly rhythm. Quarterly is a great rhythm, by the way. It is a long enough time between distributions that you start looking forward to them, anticipating them. But it isn't so frequent that they come to feel like a normal part of your personal income.

If your company has multiple owners, the distributed profit is divided up based on the percentage owned by each equity owner. If you own 60 percent of the company, another partner owns 35 percent, and an angel investor owns 5 percent, the distribution on the PROFIT account with a $5000 balance would be $2,500 total. $1,500 (for you, the 60 percent owner), $875 (for the 35 percent person) and $125 (for the investor).

The key is this: the profit distribution can *never* go back to the company. You can't use a fancy term like *reinvest, plowback, or profit retention*. No term you use will cover up the fact that you are stealing from Peter to pay Paul. Your business needs to run off the money it generates in its operating expenses. The plowback of profit means you aren't operating efficiently enough to run off the operating expenses. And if you give the profit back, you won't experience the very important reward of your company serving you. So always take your profit, every quarter, and use it for your own purposes. It's celebration time!

REWARDS AND CELEBRATIONS

OWNING A PROFIT FIRST COMPANY has its rewards. There isn't much difference between the profit distribution process that Mike describes and what I recommend. Let me outline the one distinction. Many of my clients do not have a three-month reserve in place for their operating expenses. They don't have a reserve for payroll either. Ecommerce businesses should take a less aggressive distribution approach initially, until the reserves are established and funded. Instead of taking half of the profit account balance on the first day of the quarter, I suggest taking half of the funds added to the profit account during the quarter on the first day of the new quarter. You still get a sizable reward for your risk as a business owner.

Here's an example: You have a balance of $5000 in your profit account on day one of the new quarter. On day one of the previous quarter, your balance was $3000. So, in the quarter just completed, you added $2000 to your account. Instead of taking $2500, or half of the account balance ($5,000/2= $2,500), take $1000, which is half of the amount you accumulated during the quarter ($2,000/2= $1,000). That will leave your balance in the profit account at $4000. You can see that, using my method, the profit account grows faster. It's my objective to get my clients to a safe level as quickly as possible. Once we are at this level, we have some decisions to make. Do we go to Mike's method, or do we continue to grow that profit account and ultimately grow the vault account?

The fun part is about to begin! So, what do you do with your half? Go on a family vacation? Or buy that cool car you've been dreaming of? Carole had fun close to home with her distributions. "With my first one, I went to an upscale grocery store and treated myself to fancy sauces, spices, and other goodies that I'd normally consider a splurge. I used another one to upgrade some of the items I chose when we remodeled our master bathroom."

Jeremy is pretty practical too. "I like to do things like buying stocks and building balances in my daughter's braces subaccount," he said. "My wife has a quarterly goal of having a spa day that she uses some of her bonus for. And we usually get a babysitter and go out on a nice dinner date."

For Mark, living in Thailand means attending to different practicalities. "I have taken money out of the profit account to buy a business in Thailand to secure renewable visas for living here. Living full-time in this beautiful country can be a hassle, given the political climate. People need to go in and out of the country regularly to renew their visas or they need to take Thai language classes to qualify for education visas, etc. It's always a hustle. I decided to buy into a business that provides both my wife and me with business visas and work permits as long as we keep the business running."

DEBT REDUCTION

Now, profit distribution requires a different strategy if you have debt in your business. In that case, what works is a three-pronged approach.

Your priority is to freeze the debt, to stop it from growing. In fact, try to reduce your expenses so you are under the operating expense level from your profit assessment by at least 10 percent.

Next, you want to begin paying down that debt using your quarterly profit distribution. Pick between the approaches outlined by Mike and me, above. Mike's way will eliminate your debt faster; my way is slower, but it will build more quickly for a rainy day. Either approach can work, depending upon your situation. Often, banking cash for an impending challenge is required alongside debt reduction. Remember, most companies, even profitable ones, go out of business because they are out of cash. I'm biased in favor of my approach for this reason.

TAKE ACTION

DECIDE TODAY HOW YOU WILL use your profit distribution! Email me at Cyndi@ProfitFirstEcom.com and let me know your plan for that money!

CHAPTER SEVEN

Your Life, Reverse Engineered

ONE OF THE UNEXPECTED BENEFITS of Profit First is that you can use the system to work backwards, reverse engineering your business and ultimately your personal income. When Jeremy contacted me a few years ago, this was his goal. He wanted to make the business work to support the personal income he needed, so he asked me to help him get started with Profit First. His goal was to leave his day job without risking his family's financial health.

We talked about how we could use Profit First to achieve his goal, and we got it set up and operating smoothly. Honestly, I wanted to see how dedicated and disciplined Jeremy was about working the plan. I didn't need to be concerned. He is very motivated and detail-oriented and was executing the system flawlessly.

Then we used what we knew about his business and his personal income needs to reverse engineer his business finances. With the end numbers in mind, he set about growing his business to achieve his desired level of owner's pay.

This is the process we used to get to his goal numbers. It is not an exact science, but a process used for planning and modeling possible scenarios. (Note: We have created a calculator for you to help you do the math. After you read through this section to understand the process and the information you will need, go to www.ProfitFirstEcom.com and look for the Owner Pay Calculator. You can plug in your information there.)

Desired Personal Income	
Real Revenue Range	
Gross Margin	
Top Line Revenue	
Inventory	
Real Revenue	
Profit	
Owner's Pay	
Tax	
Operating Expenses	

First, we start with this chart from Profit First that outlines the finances of a healthy business. If you know your real revenue amount, then, using the information from this chart, you can start to make some assumptions.

	A	B	C	D	E	F
Real Revenue Range	$0 - $250k	$250k - $500k	$500k - $1m	$1m - $5m	$5m - $10m	$10m - $50m
Real Revenue	100%	100%	100%	100%	100%	100%
Profit	5%	10%	15%	10%	15%	20%
Owner's Pay	50%	35%	20%	10%	5%	0%
Tax	15%	15%	15%	15%	15%	15%
Operating Expenses	30%	40%	50%	65%	65%	65%

If you haven't completed the profit assessment from Chapter Two, doing that exercise will make this process more meaningful because you can have confidence in your starting assumptions. If you want to take a shortcut, look at your P&L and use your gross profit (sales less COGS); it will get you close.

The other starting information you need is your income requirements for your personal life. What does it cost you to support yourself or your family? Take off those rose-colored glasses and be realistic in making this projection!

Let's work through a couple of scenarios. If you know you're going to need a personal income of $75,000, for example, and you know your business is operating in the real revenue range of $0–$250K (column A), you can calculate the rest of the chart. If you have your finances in order and know your gross margin, you can get to your top line revenue. Let's take a look at the calculations and results using this example.

Desired owner's pay for the year is $75,000. Divide that by 50 percent (from column A, row Owner's Pay), the portion of owner's pay you can expect with a business that has a real revenue in the range of $0–$250K.

$$75,000 / 50\% = \$150,000$$

To achieve a $75,000 salary, real revenue must be $150,000. Knowing that you must achieve real revenue of $150,000, you can complete the chart and align your business with these percentages:

$150,000 * 5% for profit = $7,500
$150,000 * 50% for owner's pay = $75,000
$150,000 * 15% for taxes = $22,500
$150,000 * 30% for operating expenses = $45,000

To complete the picture, you need to determine your top line revenue and inventory and selling fees. This will require that you have a good handle on your financials. Look at your historical gross margins (gross profit/revenue) * 100. For our example, let's assume you have a 34 percent gross margin. Divide your real revenue ($150,000, in our example) by your gross margin (34 percent), and the result is your top line revenue.

$150,000 / 34% = $441,200 approximate top line revenue.

This is where you do your reality check. Can you achieve that level of sales? Are you confident in your gross margin percentage? Please don't pull this number out of your inventory tracking system unless you have verified it against your financial statements.

As an aside, most inventory management software systems that we see our clients use are open systems which, again, do not reconcile back to bank and credit card account statements. When we build books for our clients, we often see huge discrepancies between the numbers from these systems and the books we create. The problem is not with the software, but the fact that the cost data that is added in has no way of being verified. Costs change; you must continually update this information. You can't set it and forget it. If your inventory planning system gives you a number that correlates to your financial system, you're getting it right.

How much cash will it take to buy inventory to achieve these sales? You may have to adjust your desired pay or look for products with higher margins. The point is to understand your numbers and to build a model that you know works. Once you have done this, you can determine which variables can be adjusted to get your desired results. Don't gloss over this step; your family's future depends on you getting it right.

Once you get your results, you will likely be paying more in operating expenses because you haven't been paying yourself. You need to start course corrections now to move toward the percentages recommended in the chart. The money to pay you has to come from somewhere. Typically, it's from reducing operating expenses. Another area to address is your product costs. Are you getting the best deals? Is your gross margin above 30 percent with all your products, or are some of your products taking your cash and failing to perform? Is your inventory turning? All the inventory factors we discussed in Chapter Three must be dialed in.

Armed with the results from this type of business analysis, Jeremy began to dedicate funds to grow his owner's pay account. Up until that point, he had invested his profits from the business back into the company because he could rely on financial support from his day job. He is analytical by nature, and watched his personal expenses to understand what he had to cover with a salary from the business; he also watched the owner's pay account grow to see if it was big enough. He analyzed this for six months, until he and his wife were confident that the new income level from the business would work and that he had enough in the owner's pay account to supplement those months when it didn't.

Here is how Jeremy describes it: "For two to two and a half years, I was working my day job and the Amazon business with my wife. Ecommerce was my early morning, lunch, and evening job. For us, my day job income was such that I didn't need to touch the Amazon income. I think that was probably helpful.

"When you are doing a product launch, your payback period is a little way out there, especially with the pricing competition going on now. You are looking at four to six months before you've recouped your initial investment, and sometimes longer. We were able to front-load all that stuff so the products began working for us. The flywheel on the product cycle was running by itself, [with each additional product] just compounding on top of each other. That was a big reason I burned the midnight oil and hustled hard for the first stretch while I had the day job. Who knew... investing lots of time and hard work is actually the recipe.

"When I was getting to the point of transition, to leave my day job and work in the business full-time, we actually practiced. I started working with you and bookskeep at the end of the year in anticipation of the next June leaving my day job. I practiced for a number of months. We did the percentages in December, and I was following the process for the months up until the point I left my job in June.

"We were just building up the owner's pay until it ended up being almost a windfall when we finally decided we'd start taking a payout from the account. I could see: This is money coming in, money coming out on the personal side. This is owner's pay going in and going out. There was some comfort, and I could see that the business might actually work. That's when we pulled that trigger and finally we put it into action. I jumped ship from my day job in June."

Jeremy's transition went smoothly, overall. The big expenses were covered, though there were some small things he had to work out. "There is minor stuff when you have a company that is paying you a W-2 income," he explained. "Your salary is not actually their final cost. You know, the health insurance, life insurance, and all the extras that don't seem like much but can add up. The 401k matches, all that good stuff. You don't actually think about the fact that there's extra stuff beyond your salary."

REVERSE ENGINEERING PRODUCT LAUNCHES

THE FUN THING FOR ME, when I'm fortunate enough to work with creative and analytical folks like Jeremy, is that they teach me something new. Jeremy was off and doing well with his business, and we hadn't been in touch for several months, when he asked if I could do a webinar on Profit First for his mastermind group. I was happy to share the Profit First message and hoped to help someone have an easier time of managing cash flow. I didn't expect to learn from Jeremy that day.

As I mentioned in the presentation that several clients use an advanced account to prepare for product launches, Jeremy spoke up and said he actually used Profit First to reverse engineer his product launch decisions. I was intrigued by his method, and he was gracious enough to share it. He has allowed me to share his spreadsheets to make it easy for you to do your own Profit First product launch. Look for the link to them at the end of this chapter in the Take Action section.

Remember in Chapter Four, when we talked about the primacy effect? Remember sales – profit = expenses? Jeremy is using that strategy here. When Jeremy is ready to launch a new product, he begins his analysis with two pieces of information: the expected sales price of the product to the consumer and the profit percentage (and dollar amount) required to make all the work of launching the product worthwhile. Then he subtracts the desired profit from the expected price. What remains is the budget to get the product made and ready for market.

Armed with this information, Jeremy starts working with suppliers to see if they can meet his budget. He gets prices on packaging and shipping and estimates the Amazon fees based on the size and weight of the product. If the numbers come back good, he takes the next step. If not, he passes. He has realized from experience—after becoming attached to a product, preparing an analysis that didn't look good, and moving ahead anyway—that numbers don't lie. He should have passed. Now he doesn't let the emotional appeal of a project outweigh his data.

"It stinks to do all that work and stop short," Jeremy elaborated. "A couple of products have come through this process and are close, but the numbers aren't as good as we want. We're so close to placing an order and I know in my gut it doesn't feel good—and the numbers agree with my gut. Even though we spent the money on the sample fees and we have our logo on these things and we're ready to go, I know when we shouldn't move forward.

"Even though we've already sunk cost and some time, sometimes the best decision is to stop. I think this process has saved us, a number of times, from pulling the trigger on stuff and saying, 'I'll just make it work.' You need to look at your facts, not just a feeling that it's all going to work out."

Jeremy created a fantastic spreadsheet that he uses to evaluate a variety of factors that influence his purchasing decisions. He's been generous enough to share this amazing tool that can help you ensure your inventory is acquired, shipped, and stored at rates that still let you turn a profit. Take a look at this spreadsheet work of art!

Date............

Product Name _____

Per Unit Calculations

Description	Amount	Pct of Price
Sales Price	$19.99	

Profit Target

Profit (P)	$	%
Profit	$5.00	25.0%
P Subtotal	$5.00	25.0%

Expenses

Referral & Fulfillment (RF)	$	%
Referral	$3.00	15.0%
FBA Fulfillment	$4.71	23.6%
RF Subtotal	$7.71	38.6%

Advertising & Admin & Other (AAO)	$	%
PPC Unit Spend	$2.00	10.0%
Returns/Refund Fees	$0.25	1.3%
Financing/Bank Fees	$0.00	0.0%
Unknown	$0.25	1.3%
AAO Subtotal	$2.50	12.5%

FBA Shipping + Storage (S$)	$	%
Monthly Storage	$0.15	0.8%
Inbound Shipping	$0.30	1.5%
Inventory Placement	$0.40	2.0%
S$ Subtotal	$0.85	4.3%

RF AAO S$ Subtotal	$11.06	55.32%

Profit

Target	$5.00	25.0%
Actual	$3.43	17.2%
O/U	-$1.57	-7.8%

MANUF C

Target	$3.93	19.7%
Actual	$5.50	27.5%
O/U	-$1.57	-7.8%

Order		1000 Qty
Sales		$19,990.00
Profit		$3,431.50
ROI		62.4%
Months Supply*	(*100% Scale)	11.1

Monthly		
Sales		$1,799.10
Profit		$308.84

Creative is Included

Manufacturing + Freight (MANUF)

Product Name			
Order Quantity	1000		
Unit Price	$3.70		
Factory Cost at 1000 Units:		18.5%	$3,700.00

Extras

TBD	$0.30	1.5%	$300.00
Poly Bag	$0.00	0.0%	$0.00
N/A	$0.00	0.0%	$0.00
N/A	$0.00	0.0%	$0.00
N/A	$0.00	0.0%	$0.00
Extras Subtotal	$0.30	1.5%	$300.00
Extras at 1000 Units:			$300.00
COGS	$4.00		$4000.00

Freight + Customs

Freight	$0.50	2.5%	$500.00
Customs	$0.00	0.0%	$0.00
Box/Pallet Labels	$0.00	0.0%	$0.00
N/A	$0.00	0.0%	$0.00
N/A	$0.00	0.0%	$0.00
Freight + Customs Subtotal	$0.50	2.5%	$500.00
Freight Cost at 1000 Units:			$500.00

MANUF Subtotal	$4.50	22.5%	
Total MANUF Cost at 1000 Units:			$4,500.00

Creative (C)

Creative	$1.00	5.0%	$1,000
C Subtotal	$1.00	5.0%	
Creative Cost at 1000 Units:			$1,000.00

MANUF C Subtotal	$5.00	27.51%	
Total MANUF Cost at 1000 Units:			$5,500.00

Breakeven Volume (BEV)

Unit Quantity	1,000
Revenue Per Unit	$19.99
Unit Fixed (MANUF C)	$5.50
Unit Variable (RF AAO SS)	$11.06
Total Fixed Investment	$5,500.00
Contribution Margin	$8.93
Breakeven Volume (Units)	616

61.60% of total units

Payback Period

Daily Sales Estimate	3
Monthly Sales Estimate	90

Multiplier? 1

M	Scale Sales	Units/M	Cumulative	Payback
1	25%	23	23	
2	35%	32	55	
3	50%	45	100	
4	75%	68	168	
5	80%	72	240	
6	90%	81	321	
7	100%	90	411	
8	100%	90	501	
9	100%	90	591	
10	100%	90	681	Yes!
11	100%	90	771	Yes!
12	100%	90	861	Yes!

TAKE ACTION

How much cash do you need out of your business? Determine the personal budget you need to support your lifestyle, and your family's. Then reverse engineer your business to achieve that goal. We made a spreadsheet to help you. You can download it at www.ProfitFirstEcom. com.

When you're ready to evaluate your next product, download Jeremy's spreadsheet at www.ProfitFirstEcom. com. Take your profit first, and then make a good business decision based on the product and launch data.

CHAPTER EIGHT

Where It All Falls Apart: Problems You May Encounter

IN MIKE'S FIRST EDITION OF *Profit First*, he discusses a range of problems that you may run into as you implement this new way of doing business. All of the issues Mike discusses in Profit First apply to ecommerce sellers, and I have included them at the end of this chapter. My years of experience with ecommerce clients, though, have taught me that ecommerce sellers do face some unique issues, and we're going to examine those first.

FINDING AFFORDABLE BANK ACCOUNTS

SETTING UP THE ADDITIONAL PROFIT First business bank accounts can be challenging because some ecommerce sellers live outside of the US, and banking changes may require you to visit a physical bank. In addition, simply finding a bank that has affordable fees is not easy. Many of our ecommerce clients are mobile. They may be in and out of the US sporadically. They chose this business for the flexibility and ability to be location-independent.

Opening business bank accounts is a challenge even if you live in the US. For example, the paperwork required from your operating agreement is not always right at hand. Many times, your local bank, one with which you already have a relationship, will provide the kind of assistance you need to get new accounts set up when you are not able to visit their location.

As you will be opening five, seven, or even nine accounts, you want to ensure that the bank is not going to charge you a high fee for those accounts. Many banks offer packages of multiple accounts for businesses. Most commonly, I have seen a primary and secondary checking account and a savings account. Often you can negotiate and get additional accounts based on maintaining a minimum or average balance. Minimum balance requirements can be a challenge at first, but will become less of an issue as you build up your profit account balance and the reserves in your owner's pay and operating expense accounts. Many of my clients work with local credit unions that offer them a package at a minimal fee. I suggest you shop around and look for hidden fees. I'm currently seeing banks advertising no monthly fees, but they do charge for services such as connecting to your accounting software.

You may be tempted to try to game the system by keeping all of your money in one account and simply moving funds on paper. Don't do it. You monitor your bank accounts daily. This is the instant information you need to keep the system working. Moving money on paper in a spreadsheet or in your chart of accounts is not the same. It will not be kept up-to-date. You will not look at it regularly; it will simply be an added bookkeeping chore that provides no value. I know this because, as bookkeeper, I tried to implement Profit First this way. I bought into the overall concept, but thought that I was so good with QuickBooks Online that I didn't need to do it at the bank. It simply didn't work. It was never current because it didn't have to be. I never looked at it because it wasn't real.

When you set up those bank accounts, you change your spending patterns to use the accounts. It is real, and the bank accounts give you the data directly. If I couldn't do it on paper, I honestly don't believe anyone can.

REPAYING LOANS

IF YOU—LIKE MANY PEOPLE—HAVE LOANS when you begin working Profit First, that means you'll be paying for past inventory and purchases as well as current purchases. This can be challenging if your margins are low. Don't try to be too aggressive with your allocation percentages until you have paid back these loans. We want to set you up for success. Just moving money into an account only to raid it later in the month is not the objective. First, examine your margins and get real about the profitability of your business at the gross margin level. The Profit First allocations are based on real revenue, and if your margins are unhealthy, there is no or little real revenue to allocate. This is typically a big reason your business has loans in the first place. Profit First accounts will not solve this problem; they will shine a spotlight on it. You have to do the hard work of getting a product mix with margins that will allow you to operate debt-free.

UNDERESTIMATING TAX LIABILITY

VISIT WITH YOUR CPA AND project your tax liability in the third quarter. It is likely you visited with your CPA in the first quarter and were set up with estimated taxes at that time. Most likely, you have grown during the year, and you need to understand if you are on track with the year's taxes. As you discuss your year-to-date financial history, plan for your Q4 sales, too. This can be challenging if, as a seasonal business, a significant percentage of your annual revenue comes in Q4.

If you are skimping on your tax account allocation during the year, adjust it for Q4 and get up to that 15 percent if possible. Q4 is when you will most likely have the most cash flowing through your business. It is better to set aside the funds for taxes when those funds are available, and not in March when sales are at their slowest and you may be placing down payments on inventory purchases for next year's Q4 boom.

INVENTORY INSANITY REVISITED

"IF I JUST HAVE MORE inventory, I can have the cash flow I need to sustain my business." It is such a common myth; I hear it over and over again. It may be true if you have worked out all the efficiencies and have your gross margins dialed in, but unfortunately, I find most new clients aren't even sure what is driving their gross margin. Then their operating expenses spin out of control when they attempt to support scaling the business for all the new inventory. Or their advertising isn't working like it used to because of an algorithm change at Amazon or Google. Or the market has simply moved on and that product isn't hot anymore. Putting borrowed money into inventory is risky and expensive. Get your business working efficiently before you take on the additional debt.

COMMON PITFALLS IN IMPLEMENTATION

Profit First works, and getting an accountability buddy will make sure you let it.

Going it alone is the biggest mistake entrepreneurs make when implementing Profit First, but there are others.

Mistake #1: Too Much Too Soon

It is extremely common for entrepreneurs new to Profit First to start putting 20 percent or even 30 percent into their PROFIT account right out of the gate. The next month they realize they can't afford it and pull the money back out to pay bills, which defeats the entire process. You must allocate profit and not touch it, so you've got to be sure that your business can handle the reduction in operating income.

To increase your profit, you need to become more efficient, to deliver the same or better results at a lower cost. Profit First works from the end goal backward. Once upon a time, you used to try to get more efficient in order to turn a profit. Now, by taking profit first, you must become efficient to support it. Same result, reverse engineered.

This is why I suggest you start with a small percentage. Don't fall into the trap of hogging all of the grub, taking too much profit up front and then shuffling most of it back into your OPERATING EXPENSES account when payroll comes due. Start with a small percentage to build the habit. Every quarter, move your Profit First allocation percentages closer to your goal by increasing them by an additional 1 or 2 percent. Starting slowly and moving slowly and deliberately will still force you to look for ways to get better and more efficient at what you do, but you won't be tempted to throw in the towel on the entire system because the pressure is too great or the task impossible.

Mistake #2: Grow First (and Profit Later)

"I like the idea of Profit First, but I want to grow my company."

This is probably the most common objection I get when I share Profit First with others. Too many entrepreneurs believe that you can have only one or the other: profit or growth. It sickens me that so many entrepreneurs think it is a tradeoff. Pick growth or pick profit, but you can't have both. Bullshit! Profit and growth go hand in hand. The healthiest companies figure out how to consistently be profitable first and then do everything to grow that.

Mistake #3: Cutting the Wrong Costs

By now you know I'm a frugality junkie. I get a high from saving money, and I get the biggest rush when I find a way to eliminate an expense altogether. Still, not all expenses should be cut. We need to invest in assets, and I define assets as things that bring more efficiency to your business by allowing you to get more results at a lower cost per result. So if an expense makes it easier to get better results, keep it or purchase it.

Money is made by efficiency—invest in it. If a purchase will bring up your bottom line and create significant efficiency, find ways to cut costs elsewhere, and consider different or discounted equipment (or resources, or services) rather than sacrifice efficiency for what you think are savings.

Mistake #4: "Plowing Back" and "Reinvesting"

We use fancy terms to justify taking money out of our different allocation accounts to cover expenses. Two that are used most often are *plowback* and *reinvest*, which are really just other ways to say borrow. I have done this. I "plowed back" money from my PROFIT account to cover operating expenses, and boy, do I regret it.

When you don't have enough money in your OPERATING EXPENSES account to cover expenses, it is a big red flag that your expenses are too high and you need to find a way to fix them fast. Once in a blue moon, it could also mean that you are allocating too much to Owner's Comp or Profit. This only happens when you start with a high Profit or Owner's Comp percentage. And when it happens, it is because you are taking a percentage of profit or pay that you are not yet able to sustain; the efficiencies are not yet in place to support your profitability. But again, this is rarely the reason your OPERATING EXPENSES account is in the red.

Likewise, some entrepreneurs continue to use their credit cards for day-to-day operations and call them lines of credit. This is not accurate. It's money you don't have. Your credit card spending limit is almost never a bridge loan to carry the business for short cash flow gaps (e.g., big profitable job isn't paying the bill on time as was committed to). Nope. Credit cards are simply to use to pay expenses, resulting in debt, plain and simple. Using a credit card to cover what you can't afford is also a red flag that your expenses are too high. Stop using the credit card and reserve it for legitimate emergencies or unique circumstances (like for a purchase you must make to yield income).

When you find yourself in a situation where you feel the need to "plow back" your profits, *stop* to reassess. There is always a better, more sustainable way to maintain the health of your business. You need to invest thought, not reinvest money.

Mistake #5: Raiding the Tax Account

In the first year or two of doing Profit First, you may get caught in a tax bind because you only pay your estimates. For example, your accountant may prepare estimates based on your business's prior year's income and profitability that say you should make payments of $5,000 every quarter.

As your PROFIT account and TAX account grow, you may be surprised to see that you're reserving about $8,000 in taxes each quarter. Seeing this, you might think, "Hey, my accountant said I should pay $5,000 per quarter. I'm reserving too much for taxes." A little voice inside your head may even say, "Don't touch that money; you'll probably need it for taxes." And then a louder voice will say, "Nah, don't worry about it; you probably won't owe it and even if you do, you have time."

As your profitability grows, your taxes will, too. In fact, paying more taxes is an indicator that your business health is improving. Now, I am not saying you should ever pay more taxes than you need to (tax is just an expense like any other), but do realize that your taxes will grow as your business health does. So don't steal from your TAX account thinking you won't need that money for taxes. You will.

At times, you may even need more than you think. One year I messed up when I paid my estimated taxes every quarter and then used the extra money to increase my Owner's Comp when I discovered there was money left over. Dummy! Tax estimates are based on your prior year's income. If you make more profit this year (which you will), you will pay more taxes, but your tax *estimates* will not change. If you spend "leftover" money from your TAX account simply because you allocate more than the estimate, you will be in shock come tax time.

Talk to an accountant who specializes in *both* profit maximization and tax minimization (if you are unsure whether they do, ask them to share their method*) every quarter to gauge how you are doing on taxes. And don't take money out of that TAX account! Your business is growing by leaps and bounds, and higher taxes are definitely in your future.

Another tax issue has to do with paying down debt. I call this paying for your sins because if you have debt you need to wipe out, implementing Profit First is going to hurt in the beginning. I should know—it happened to me.

Here's the problem: the government gives you a tax break on expenses but does not consider the money you reserve to pay down debt an expense. The actual charges on your credit card and the interest and credit card fees can be expensed, but not your payments to pay down your cards.

I can't believe I'm saying this, but in this case, the government is right. You get the tax benefit in the year that you make the purchase—no matter if you paid for the expense in cash, by credit card or with funds from a bank loan or line of credit. As you become profitable and pay off debt, you will pay taxes on that income. Eliminating debt and paying taxes will feel like a double whammy. It isn't—you just need to pay for your "sins."

Mistake #6: Adding Complexity

As Profit First grew in popularity, I found a completely unexpected failure point: people think it needs to be more complex. It is a weird phenomenon, but many entrepreneurs are so used to struggling with accounting details that they feel they need to struggle with Profit First. And if they are not struggling, they think something must be wrong. So they just make up rules to add confusion. I know this sounds odd, but I have seen it happen time and time again.

I have seen entrepreneurs modify their bank balances by introducing depreciation or amortization of stuff. Don't do this. Cash is cash. Either you have it or you don't.

I have seen entrepreneurs take a profit distribution, put it in their savings, then pay for a purchase or make a hire with the money and say it is not an expense because it came out of their pocket. Ahhh! That is a shell game. And it is an expense. Profit is a reward (in the form of a cash distribution) for the equity owners of the business, and is above and beyond their pay from working in the business (Owner's Comp).

The system is super easy. It has been designed to work with how you naturally work; hence it is fluid. Don't overthink it. Don't add complexity. Don't try to "outsmart" the system. Just get comfortable with the fact that sometimes getting the results you want is way easier to achieve than all the hard work you have put in to get the results you don't want.

Mistake #7: Skipping the Bank Accounts

Some folks try to "simplify" Profit First by not setting up the bank accounts. They just have their bookkeeper manage it. They are entrepreneurs, after all, and don't have the time for "unnecessary" nuances. So they use a spreadsheet or modify the chart of accounts in their accounting system to emulate the Profit First "small plate" bank accounts. Then, immediately, Profit First fails to work. When this happens, they blame the system, but the problem is they didn't *use* the system.

Profit First must be set up to be directly in the path of the natural behavior of you, the entrepreneur. Because you log on to your bank account to look at your balance and make decisions, you must have Profit First there. Spreadsheets of your accounting system's general ledger reports are great, but they are also too late. You don't look at them when making in-the-moment money decisions; you look at them after the fact. Coming up with a battle plan after the battle is over is useless.

Profit First at the bank will be in your face every time you look at the accounts, enabling you to manage profitability and cash flow decisions in real time. Setting up your accounts means you can't avoid it, and that is exactly how it needs to be.

Profit First is set up so that even those of us who don't happen to be rocket scientists can train ourselves to become the owners of profitable businesses. The process works best when you don't clutter it up with unnecessary frills, but follow the steps as they're written, especially at the start. Oh, and don't worry...if you do happen to be a rocket scientist, Profit First will work for you, too!

TAKE ACTION

FIND YOURSELF AN ACCOUNTABILITY PARTNER. Make sure that person shares the same mindset about how to grow your business organically and will talk you down from that inventory purchase when it is not the right time. If you don't know anyone, email me now at Cyndi@ ProfitFirstEcom.com. I'll connect you with a client or two that may be a good fit.

CHAPTER NINE

Welcome to Ecommerce Prosperity!

Now you know that your business is like everyone else's business. We have all struggled with cash flow at some point. We have all faced that elephant in the room. As business owners, we must acknowledge stark realities and take steps that will move us in the right direction. You now have the tools to take these steps.

Profitability is closer than you think; you simply must take action. This week I had three calls in one day with clients who have all turned a corner. They started with terrible debt crises and can now see their way out. Systematically, they raised prices, negotiated for better deals with shippers, cut expenses, cut products that weren't profitable, and cut advertising dollars that didn't generate cash in their bank accounts. They all started by committing to resolve the issues, and by taking the first simple step of opening two new bank accounts for inventory and profit.

Make it a new habit to fund those accounts for the next three months. Once you start, your business will be profitable by default because you have money in your profit account. It's a bold new approach that you will find rewarding, and it will push you to improve. In addition, you will be able to see more clearly where to focus your energy so you can get to work on the other challenges. You can do this! Mark, Carole, and Jeremy did, and so can you!

When we met Mark, he really didn't understand his financials. He was stuck in the maze. His books were being maintained by a CPA, but they were a mess. He wanted to get organized and understand his inventory. Now, two and a half years later, his business has grown to the point where we are helping him prepare it for sale. We are working with his business broker to ensure that the formatting and presentation of the numbers align with buyer's preferences in evaluation and performance of due diligence. Mark and his business have come a long way in a short time because he took action.

Jeremy had his financials in pretty good order, but he was going to take a big step and leave his day job. We helped him implement Profit First, and in six months he made that step with confidence. He has been his own boss for over a year, and his business is growing. He is enjoying new flexibility that allows him to spend more time with his wife and children and even make trips to see extended family across the country. This is possible because he took action and made that bold and calculated leap.

Carole took action because she wanted to understand her numbers. She was ready to dial in her business, but there was too much inconsistency in her books. Once her financials were in order and her systems humming, she landed on a product that had significant sales last summer. Understanding her numbers allowed her to make good decisions as she rode the wave of that product's growth.

Carole told me, "The thing that I like best about Profit First is that I feel really confident in knowing where my business stands financially. I'm not fretting over whether I'm about to go under.

There's no wondering. Everything is very clear. Where the money is going is very clear. I would imagine the people who only have one account don't really know how they're spending their money. Because if they've got inventory, expenses, payroll, taxes, and owner's pay, all coming out of a single account, they have no idea what portion of the whole each one of those represents. Whether you're being efficient or not, and whether you're overspending or underspending in a particular category, it's a lot harder to break it out."

Mark said, "The easiest benefit to put into words, as I explained to my Million Dollar Seller group, is I know where my cash goes. I know how much marketing costs in general, and probably a lot more specifically than most people, because when you set up your Profit First accounts, you specify the percentages allocated to each account. And to carry that forward, if I make changes in my marketing spend, if I get more efficient or maybe I get more bloated, I know. I know what's happening. I can see. Maybe I'm running out of my budget that I set aside, while last year I was hitting my budget every time. What's changed? These are things that you might not notice if you just kept one big bank account, unless you had a CFO who was running these kinds of spreadsheets and numbers for you. Most businesses my size can't afford to get the bird's eye view of where all the money goes at any time of the day."

And Jeremy said, "Before my call with you, my wife and I were having an intense conversation about life. Where do we want to live? Should we move? Should we do this or that? Should we try traveling for a little while? As we're talking, I'm thinking, how's this going to impact my owner's pay, percentages? Is this gonna work? It's amazing how some recent health issues with extended family puts that in perspective. Overall, it's good because we only have one shot at this life and it's nice to be able to make informed decisions for yourself. I attribute a lot of that to the methodical nature of Profit First. It really helps. I'm not just saying that to you because we're talking about it, it really just helps."

Now it's your turn to act! Set up your inventory and profit bank accounts today! It really is that easy to start.

ADDENDUM ONE

Top Accounting Techniques
of Profit First Ecommerce Sellers

What makes an online retail business different for financial management? Cloud software technology! Our ecommerce sellers are sophisticated software and systems users. These tools can be helpful in your Profit First implementation.

Accounting Tools

While Profit First can be used with just your bank accounts, we think a business needs more robust data, especially with accounting for inventory. We recommend either QuickBooks Online (QBO) or Xero for our clients. Both work well and, as cloud-based systems, provide you and your team with the flexibility to work easily from any location.

Both QBO and Xero work well; if you are used to one, I wouldn't change it. There are no overwhelming advantages to switching. If you are selecting one to start with, here are a few considerations. Both integrate with A2X (and I'll discuss A2X separately). Both integrate with most bank and credit cards and effectively address multicurrency. We like the tool in QBO that allows us to easily reconcile our registers with our bank balances. It makes it easier to find errors. We also like the reporting flexibility in QBO over Xero. This is mainly a style and familiarity perspective, but we think QBO is more intuitive for a new user. Finally, check in with your CPA. If they access your books online, they may have a preference about the system you choose.

Occasionally we are asked to work with systems like GoDaddy or other pseudo-accounting systems that integrate with Amazon. If the system you are considering does not have a balance sheet, I would not depend on it as an accounting system. The reason accounting systems are reliable is their ability to reconcile back to statements from your financial institutions. You must be able to track and reconcile your bank, credit card, and loan statements, and track your other assets such as inventory.

Sales Channels

Most of our clients sell on Amazon and Shopify. Many also sell on eBay, Etsy, Walmart, Jet, and others. There are tools available that will integrate these sales channels with your accounting system. Our experience is that the integrations at the time of this writing are not robust enough to record your accounting properly, with one exception, A2X, which I explain in detail below.

The data coming into your accounting system should be at the summary level. If you record every transaction detail, you will basically be creating a duplicate system and the accounting system will be overloaded with transactional data that will cause it to slow over time. In addition, maintaining detail level data in two systems is inefficient and can lead to errors between the systems. This leads to low confidence in the data in either system.

There is one integration that we do recommend, and that is A2X.

A2X properly integrates Amazon with QBO and Xero, with a summary level entry for each payout. A2X can handle the

Amazon sale summary information appropriately as it maps to your chart of accounts. Another benefit of using A2X is that it records your sales data using an accrual method. This helps to smooth your data out month by month instead of staying at the biweekly payout time frames. In addition, if you ever decide to sell your business, your broker or potential buyer will want your sales and COGS set up on an accrual method in order to conduct their due diligence assessment.

Finally, if you can maintain a spreadsheet or export your product cost list from an inventory system into a spreadsheet, you can upload these costs into A2X and it will also make the journal entry for you to record your costs of goods sold. This works well for our clients, and we recommend A2X without hesitation.

Inventory Systems

There are several good, affordable inventory systems that integrate with Amazon. If you are just getting started or have a small number of SKUs, you can use spreadsheets. Jeremy has graciously shared the forms he uses to track inventory and to plan inventory restocking. These are found as downloads at www.ProfitFirstEcom.com. The monthly prices for these systems range from $40 to thousands of dollars. Obviously, you will want to evaluate the features you need and choose one that is affordable for your business.

Many people want the inventory system to integrate with QBO. In my experience, that's a mistake. And based on the products and processes we see in the marketplace, it is not an appropriate place for integration and automation. Inventory systems are typically managed by purchasing and warehouse personnel. You don't want an error introduced in that system to be automatically carried over into your financial system. You need two numbers out of your inventory system per month. It is super easy to run a report and add that information into your accounting system as a journal entry. This will save you many headaches.

Inventory tracking can get complicated, with items in a local warehouse, items in transit, and items that are prepaid. If your costs of goods sold are not making sense, consider these factors that may impact the balance in your inventory account.

Take the time to investigate your tools and choose the ones that will allow you to grow efficiently. With Profit First, we want to ensure you're putting your funds to good use.

Payroll and HR Systems

The solution we use with our clients is GUSTO. They make payroll easy and fun! Our clients need a solution that integrates with QBO and Xero, integrates with a variety of time tracking systems, and handles all of the new employee onboarding easily from a remote location. They also handle all of the W-2s and payments to federal and state revenue and labor agencies. GUSTO also processes contractor payments and issues 1099s. In addition, we love their worker's comp offering with which they deduct the premiums monthly and make the audit a nonevent. Add in their great customer support and you've got a solid partner for your business.

ADDENDUM TWO

Show Me the Money!

Can't you hear Cuba Gooding, Jr. saying that line? The line I commonly hear from my clients is similar: "My P&L shows I made a profit, so where's my money?" It's a common misconception that all profits lead directly to money in the bank. Let's debunk that myth and get clear on the difference between profit and cash flow.

Let's start with your bottom line. Looking at your P&L (profit and loss statement, or income statement) you will see your net income or net profit. That is the amount you have left from your sales after you pay for the products you sold and cover the expenses to run your business. This is the number many business owners equate with cash in the bank.

To get a true picture of your cash, you need to look at your balance sheet too. The balance sheet is a summary of your business over its lifetime. It is more than the current year's information. If you want to understand how your balance sheet has changed over time, I recommend printing out the balance sheet from the last date of business for the prior year. For example, December 31, 2017 would be the date for most businesses operating on a calendar-year basis. Then print the balance sheet for the current year-to-date. Compare the bank account balances from last year to this year's. Do you have more money or less? Let's assume your cash increased. There's my money, right? Not so fast.

You must also look at your liabilities. Liabilities is the big word for money you owe. If you have Amazon or Kabbage loans and credit card debt, this means that you were spending someone else's money instead of your cash. To understand more of this story, do the same exercise for liabilities and compare last year's liabilities balance to your current liabilities balance. Do you owe more than last year? For our example, let's assume you owe less.

Now you need to compare the difference in your cash to the difference in your liabilities. Let's say your cash went up and your liabilities went down—that's the good news story. It also tells you that some of that bottom line money went to pay down debt.

Another scenario is that your cash went up and your liabilities did too. That situation means you are using someone else's money to pay for expenses and your cash increased.

Finally, the sad news story is that your cash decreased *and* your debt increased. In that case, your P&L may show a negative bottom line. Your business is in trouble and you need to get control of your income and/or expense side of your P&L.

The final area you need to examine is the equity section of balance sheet. Most small businesses will have owner or partner contribution and distribution accounts. Compare these accounts from last year-end to the current date. Did you have to add money to your business, or are you taking money out of the business? Depending on the type of entity you have, your pay may show up on the balance sheet as an owner distribution and not on the P&L report. So, if you have a P&L bottom line of $50,000 this year-to-date and you paid yourself $60,000 so far this year, your cash will go down by that amount.

When I complete a Profit First assessment, which tracks how the cash flows, I commonly see people paying themselves with their cash while all of their operating expenses are on credit cards.

This is not a healthy, sustainable business. It's a house of cards that will fold unless the business model is improved.

Below is an illustration of the reports you will need to pull from your accounting system to show you where your money goes. This illustration is for a business using the modified cash accounting method for the purpose of matching revenue and product costs. This means that inventory is recorded as an asset on the balance sheet until it is sold. Once the goods are sold, an entry is made to reduce the inventory account and record the cost of goods sold on the P&L. As the business saying goes, "Cash is king," so know where the king hangs out to get on top of your business's financial health.

This example of a profit and loss statement, or P&L, shows a net income of $15,520:

PROFIT AND LOSS
January 1 - September 12, 2018

	TOTAL
▾ Income	
▸ AMZ Product Charges	138,991.83
AMZ Vendor Express Sales	1,350.00
▸ Paypal Product Sales	3,971.91
▸ Shopify Income	6,969.05
Total Income	$151,282.79
▸ Cost of Goods Sold	$99,384.21
GROSS PROFIT	$51,898.58
▸ Expenses	$35,505.04
NET OPERATING INCOME	$16,393.54
▸ Other Income	$3.02
▸ Other Expenses	$876.28
NET OTHER INCOME	$ -873.26
NET INCOME	$15,520.28

This balance sheet report shows a column for December 31, 2017, the end of the prior year for the client, and a column for September 12, 2018, the current year-to-date information.

BALANCE SHEET
As of September 12, 2018

	DEC 31, 2017	JAN 1 - SEP 12, 2018
▼ ASSETS		
▼ Current Assets		
▸ Bank Accounts	$30,826.86	$18,753.63
▸ Accounts Receivable	$0.00	$0.00
▸ Other Current Assets	$8,182.14	$4,414.06
Total Current Assets	$39,009.00	$23,167.69
TOTAL ASSETS	$39,009.00	$23,167.69
▼ LIABILITIES AND EQUITY		
▼ Liabilities		
▼ Current Liabilities		
▸ Accounts Payable	$2,989.04	$4,934.98
▸ Credit Cards	$1,116.74	$3,105.74
▸ Other Current Liabilities	$235.75	$379.90
Total Current Liabilities	$4,341.53	$8,420.62
Total Liabilities	$4,341.53	$8,420.62
▼ Equity		
Owner Contributions	30,467.72	43,767.72
Owner Distributions	-56,493.70	-105,234.38
Owner's Equity	15,218.49	15,218.49
Retained Earnings	-5,910.33	45,474.96
Net Income	51,385.29	15,520.28
Total Equity	$34,667.47	$14,747.07
TOTAL LIABILITIES AND EQUITY	$39,009.00	$23,167.69

Quick Calculations

Bank Accounts: $18,753 - $30,826 = -12,073 (the bank account decreased)

Liability Accounts: $8,420 - $4,341 = $4,079

Owner Contributions: $43,767 - $30,467 = $13,300

Owner Distributions: $105,234 - $56,493 = $48,441

Net of Owner Contributions and Distributions: $48,441 - $13,300 = $35,141 cash reduction to the business.

Analysis

Based on the P&L statement, this business has a profit this year-to-date of $15,520. This means the business operations generated cash. When we look at the balance sheet, the cash in bank accounts has decreased and the liabilities have increased. Typically, this indicates a business that is not profitable. However, we note from the equity section that the owner has taken $35,141 out of the business this year. The cash generated from the business this year is insufficient to meet the owner's cash demands; therefore, debt has increased to meet this need. This is not a sustainable long-term approach, and the business needs to evaluate other ways to meet the cash needs of the owner.

ACKNOWLEDGMENTS

IT HAS BEEN SUCH A privilege to serve those in the ecommerce community and to learn the challenges they face in the online retail world. Writing this book has helped me to further understand their needs and how we can serve them better. I appreciate the opportunity that all my clients have given me and all the extra time they have taken to educate me on the issues they face.

A huge and special thank you to Mark Brenwall, Carole Rains, and Jeremy Gross for allowing me to share their stories. They have given me so much of their time and expertise, and responded to questions in the spirit of helping others learn and be successful. They are inspiring entrepreneurs.

Mike Michalowicz got me into all of this! I say that with extreme gratitude. *Profit First*, the book, set my business on a good financial foundation. Mike and the Profit First Professionals organization gave me the tools to grow into a niche specialization and to organize my business to run like clockwork! Mike has also been encouraging during every step of this writing process, which is way outside my comfort zone.

Robyn Johnson is a fellow Profit First Professional and Amazon coach and a dear friend. She is an amazing resource to me for all things Amazon, and she was there during the call with Mike when this book idea was born. Thanks, Robyn, for always giving your best to me and to everyone in the Amazon sellers community.

My fellow Profit First Professionals - Fortress members and Mastery members - have been there to offer support all along the way. I owe Mike, the Profit First Home Base, and fellow Profit First Professionals so much. Thank you all.

Thank you, Kelsey Ayers of Profit First Professionals, for assistance with cover design, publishing, and overall coordination of this project. Thanks, Meggan Robinson, for editing this book and making it all flow. Thanks, AJ Harper, for calming my nerves and for providing the spit and polish this book needed to be more engaging. Your guidance around the publishing process and marketing programs have also been so helpful. Thanks, Zoë Bird, for your awesome job in copy editing. Thanks, Choi Messer, for making this book visually appealing with your page design and typesetting expertise. Thanks, John Stephan of MCS Studios for making the audio recording process of my book an absolute pleasure. And thank you, Amber Dugger, for being my GLAM BLAM, my glamorous book launch manager and cheerleader!

Thank you to my booksPeeps! They are on the front lines every day serving our clients. They make me look good! A special thank you to Bree Eddings, who has been by my side since the beginning to make sure the book gets out to the community it is meant to serve. You're a rock star! Thanks to honorary booksPeep, Mary Richards, for your constant encouragement and for opening your home to me as a quiet place to write.

Dave is my rock both at home and at work. He keeps things humming and grounded at home, and in the bookskeep world, he spends every day trying to bring my vision to life. Thank you so much; I can't imagine doing any of this without you. Thank you to my mom, Eleanor Potts, the real entrepreneur in the family, who taught me to just do it and never stop! And thanks to my dad,

George Small, who taught me patience and reflection. Finally, thank you to Alaina for the inspiration to dream big and tackle my goals with tenacity. I love you all so much!

bookskeep

Financial Strategy & Solutions

CONTACT US!

To ACCESS OUR RESOURCES PAGE, visit www.ProfitFirstEcom.com. If you need additional assistance with implementing Profit First, contact cyndi@ProfitFirstEcom.com.

To learn more about bookskeep and our bookkeeping services, go to www.bookskeep.com.

FOLLOW US!

- facebook.com/bookskeep
- linkedin.com/company/bookskeep

CPSIA information can be obtained
at www.ICGtesting.com
Printed in the USA
BVHW031241271020
591920BV00001B/201

9 780960 028313